BLACK MAGIC

Black Magic

Sabotage   Target Study   Black Art

Collected Poetry, 1961–1967

LeRoi Jones

THE BOBBS-MERRILL COMPANY
Indianapolis and New York

The Bobbs-Merrill Company, Inc.
A Subsidiary of Howard W. Sams & Co., Inc., Publishers
Indianapolis   Kansas City   New York

For my family

Ameena, my wife
Rashidah, my daughter
Jahidah, my daughter
Obalaji Malik Ali, my son

"Go on with your terrible selves"

Some of these poems have appeared in the following publications:

Signal   Yowl   Negro Verse   Wild Dog   Fuck You
   The Swallow   Down Beat   Niagara Frontier Review
The Nation   Matter   Revolution   Imago   "C"   Trobar
Negro Digest   Sum   Tampa Review   Poetry   Fuballo
   Red Dust   Rights and Reviews   Kulchur   Diplomat
Liberator   Streets   Harper's Magazine   Pivano Anthology
Black Dialogue   Afro American Festival of the Arts Magazine
            Paris Review   Soul Book

An Explanation of the Work

This book contains three books, *Sabotage* (1961–1963), *Target Study* (1963–1965), and *Black Art* (1965–1966). The first, *Sabotage*, picks up just after *The Dead Lecturer*. *The Dead Lecturer* picked up right after *Preface to a Twenty Volume Suicide Note*.

You notice the preoccupation with death, suicide, in the early works. Always my own, caught up in the deathurge of this twisted society. The work a cloud of abstraction and disjointedness, that was just whiteness. European influence, etc., just as the concept of hopelessness and despair, from the dead minds the dying morality of Europe. There is a spirituality always trying to get through, to triumph, to walk across these dead bodies like stuntin for disciples, walking the water of dead bodies europeans call their minds.

Sabotage meant I had come to see the superstructure of filth Americans call their way of life, and wanted to see it fall. To sabotage it, I thought maybe by talking bad and getting high, layin out on they whole chorus. But *Target Study* is trying to really study, like bomber crews do the soon to be destroyed cities. Less passive now, less uselessly "literary." Trying to see, trying to understand . . . "Will the machinegunners please step forward . . ." trying, as Margaret Walker says, "to fashion a way," to clean up and move.

Black Art was the crucial seeing, the decisions, the actual move. The strengthening to destroy, and the developing of willpower to build, even in the face of destruction and despair, even with, or WITHOUT, the confrontation of blankness, whiteness, etc. These black men floating around like chocolate bars in the cosmos eat up by beastooth waiting for some devil to hangup a painting or something, a footprint in the snow, without institutions to show themselves, without real reflectors of them, but always seeing themselves, abstracted, and halfways, cubed, squared, drawn out of shape by their constant need to relate to the devil.

We are spiritual, and we must force this issue, we must see our selves again, as black men, as the strength of the planet, and rise to rebuild what is actually spiritual, what is actually good, and leave the evil Duhevil the devil, alone, leave the filth, the freakishness, the perversion, the selfcentered unhealthy egoism, Alone, with its self. Albino doo doo in a dark auditorium.

Black Art was a beginning, a rebeginning, a coming in contact with the most beautiful part of myself, with our selves. The whole race connected in its darkness, in its sweetness. We must study each other. And for the aliens we say I aint studying you.

So Black Art opened, opens the way, for us all, if you can dig it. So in "Answers in Progress," written around the same time as "Black People" (written after '66, but thrown in cause I felt like it), we begin to look into the future, which is happening at the same instant, but further away.

My work after 1966 is self-consciously spiritual, and stronger. I leave this "poetry" at 1966 because I did not want to give the devils all of it. Jihad has the other works ready, i.e., *The Book of Life*, which is a thread of philosophy, a thread of religion, a cloth of prophecy, from the soothsayer, one flayed and shaped by evil as a fountainhead of reality finally glimpses of true airflame. We must have works of prophecy to conquer the still existing void of blankness.

As Salaam Alaikum,
Ameer Baraka

1968

Sabotage

1961–1963

Three Modes of History and Culture

Chalk mark sex of the nation, on walls we drummers
know
as cathedrals. Cathedra, in a churning meat milk.

Women glide through looking for telephones. Maps
weep
and are mothers and their daughters listening to

music teachers. From heavy beginnings. Plantations,
learning
America, as speech, and a common emptiness. Songs knocking

inside old women's faces. Knocking through cardboard trunks.
Trains
leaning north, catching hellfire in windows, passing through

the first ignoble cities of missouri, to illinois, and the panting
Chicago.
And then all ways, we go where flesh is cheap. Where factories

sit open, burning the chiefs. Make your way! Up through fog and
history
Make your way, and swing the general, that it come flash open

and spill the innards of that sweet thing we heard, and gave theory
to.
Breech, bridge, and reach, to where all talk is energy. And there's

enough, for anything singular. All our lean prophets and rhythms.
Entire
we arrive and set up shacks, hole cards, Western hearts at the edge

of saying. Thriving to balance the meanness of particular skies.
Race
of madmen and giants.

Brick songs. Shoe songs. Chants of open weariness.
Knife wiggle early evenings of the wet mouth. Tongue
dance midnight, any season shakes our house. Don't
tear my clothes! To doubt the balance of misery

ripping meat hug shuffle fuck. The Party of Insane
Hope. I've come from there too. Where the dead told lies
about clever social justice. Burning coffins voted
and staggered through cold white streets listening
to Willkie or Wallace or Dewey through the dead face
of Lincoln. Come from there, and belched it out.

I think about a time when I will be relaxed.
When flames and non-specific passion wear themselves
away. And my eyes and hands and mind can turn
and soften, and my songs will be softer
and lightly weight the air.

A Poem Welcoming Jonas Mekas To America

This night's first star, hung
high up over a factory. From my window,
a smile held my poetry in. A tower, where I work
and drink, vomit, and spoil myself for casual life.

Looking past things, to their meanings. All the pretensions
of consciousness. Looking out, or in, the precise stare
of painful reference. (Saying to the pretty girl, "Pain
has to be educational.") Or so I thought, riding down

in the capsule, call it elevator lady, speedless forceless
profile thrust toward the modern lamp, in lieu of a natural
sun. Our beings are here. (Take this chance to lick yourself,
the salt and stain of memory history and object.) Shit! Love!

Things we must have some use for. Old niggers in time on the
dreary street. Man, 50 . . . woman, 50, drunk and falling in the street.
I could say, looking at their lot, a poet has just made a note of your
hurt. First star, high over the factory. I could say, if I had any courage

but my own. First star, high over the factory. Get up off the ground, or
just look at it, calmly, where you are.

A POEM SOME PEOPLE WILL HAVE TO UNDERSTAND

Dull unwashed windows of eyes
and buildings of industry. What
industry do I practice? A slick
colored boy, 12 miles from his
home. I practice no industry.
I am no longer a credit
to my race. I read a little,
scratch against silence slow spring
afternoons.
        I had thought, before, some years ago
that I'd come to the end of my life.
        Watercolor ego. Without the preciseness
a violent man could propose.
        But the wheel, and the wheels,
wont let us alone. All the fantasy
        and justice, and dry charcoal winters
All the pitifully intelligent citizens
        I've forced myself to love.

We have awaited the coming of a natural
phenomenon. Mystics and romantics, knowledgeable
workers
of the land.

But none has come.
(*Repeat*)
            but none has come.

Will the machinegunners please step forward?

Houdini

Poured, white powder
on the back of a book
took out my plastic funnel
and honked the powder
up.

Then sit down, to write
before consciousness
drained away. Feeling
the change, the bag-like quality
of ease.

This will be
the last sense I make
for hours.

Citizen Cain

In the great northwest, always, my grandfather warned me,
cold,
and nothing but foreigners. Inexperienced dudes on trains,
and their other luxuries
like murder, and de-balling
for the young girls, teaching them mambo-fear
at tender age, for any bucks happen to make
seventeen. We string them up or out. Along
the reef of threatening waters. Call it success,
and sit in a bar under eight layers of disease.
Call it disappearance, that even the "terrorists"
shave their heads and sound like Miles Standish.

Where's it all leave me? A romantic liar, a coward, not even
the courage to kill myself, or drink myself to death. Just
be herded off like a common jew, and roasted in my teary
denunciations. I'll go to jail and become a fag, write
a huge treatise on religion, and never speak another
english word.

2.

Roi, finish this poem, someone's about to need you. Roi,
dial the mystic number, ask for holy beads, directions,
plans for the destruction of New York. Work out your problems
like your friends on some nice guy's couch. Get up and hit
someone, like you useta. Don't sit here trembling under the
hammer. Fate like a season of abstract reference. Like an
abstract execution where only ideas are shot full of holes.
Don't sit there drowned in your own bad writing Get up and
throw that ball. Move your hips, cut, like the white boys,
for ten more yards. Tackle and punch, then sit down grinning
and waiting for some Barrymore to lick you clean. Get up
and get high, so you wont understand what those gentlemen want,
spying for months from the dope factory. Ask the white man
for your passport and quit it, little jesus. Your time is up
in this particular feeling. In this particular throb of meaning.
Roi, baby, you blew the whole thing.

Letter To E. Franklin Frazier

Those days when it was all right
to be a criminal, or die, a postman's son,
full of hallways and garbage, behind the hotdog store
or in the parking lots of the beautiful beer factory.

Those days I rose through the smoke of chilling Saturdays
hiding my eyes from the shine boys, my mouth and my flesh
from their sisters. I walked quickly and always alone
watching the cheap city like I thought it would swell
and explode, and only my crooked breath could put it together
again.

By the projects and small banks of my time. Counting my steps
on tar or new pavement, following the sun like a park. I imagined
a life, that was realer than speech, or the city's anonymous
fish markets. Shuddering at dusk, with a mile or so up the hill

to get home. Who did you love
then, Mussolini? What were you thinking,
Lady Day? A literal riddle of image
was me, and my smell was a continent
of familiar poetry. Walking the long way,
always the long way, and up the steep hill.

Those days like one drawn-out song, monotonously
promising. The quick step, the watchful march march,
All were leading here, to this room, where memory
stifles the present. And the future, my man, is long
time gone.

9

THE PEOPLE BURNING

May-Day! May-Day!

—Pilot talk

They now gonna make us shut up. Ease
thru windows in eight dollar hats
sharpening their pencils on match books. List
our errors and lies, stumbling over our souls
in the dark, for the sake of unnatural advantage.

They now gonna line you up, ask you about God. Nail
your answers on the wall, for the bowling alley owners
to decide. They now gonna pretend they flowers. Snake stalked
large named vegetables, who have, if nothing else,
the title: World's Vilest Living Things.

The Dusty Hearts of Texas, whose most honest world
is the long look into darkness, sensing the glittering
affront of reason or faith or learning. Preferring
fake tiger smells rubbed on the balls, and clothes
the peasants of no country on earth would ever be
vulgar enough to wear. The legacy of diseased mediocrity.

Become an Italian or Jew. Forget the hatred of natural
insolence. The teetering sense of right, as balance, each
natural man must have. Become a Jew, and join the union,
forget about Russia or any radicalism past a hooked grin.
Become an Italian quietist in some thin veneer of reasonable
gain. Lodi, Metuchen, Valley Stream, welcomes you into its
leather ridiculousness. Forget about any anarchy except the
understandable urge to be violent, or flashy, or fast, or
heavy fisted. Sing at Radio City, but never rage at the chosen,
for they have given you the keys to their hearts. Made you
the Fridays and Saturdays of the regime, clothed you in promise
and utility, and banned your thinkers to worship the rags
of your decline.

For the Reconstruction, for the march into any anonymous America,
stretches beyond hills of newsprint, and dishonorable intention.
Forget any dignity, but that that is easily purchased. And recognized
by Episcopalians as they pay their garbage bills. The blueprint's sound.

And the nation is smaller and the loudest mouths are recognized
and stunned by the filth of their hopeless truths. (I've got to
figure this all out. Got to remember just where I came in. Freedom Suite,
some five six years ago, Rollins cradling the sun, as it rose, and we
dreamed then, of becoming, unlike our fathers, and the other cowboys,
strong men in our time, raging and clawing, at fools of any persuasion.)

Now they ask me to be a jew or italian, and turn from the moment
disappearing into the shaking clock of treasonable safety, like reruns
of films, with sacred coon stars. To retreat, and replay; throw my mind out,
sit down and brood about the anachronistic God, they will tell you
is real. Sit down and forget it. Lean on your silence, breathing
the dark. Forget your whole life, pop your fingers in a closed room,
hopped-up witch doctor for the cowards of a recent generation. It is
choice, now, like a philosophy problem. It is choice, now, and
the weight is specific and personal. It is not an emotional decision.
There are facts, and who was it said, that this is a scientific century.

Letter to Elijah Muhammad

When your talking is murdered, and only very old women
will think to give you flowers. When history is the homework
that presses you, silently, at your dying, in your blood
some briefer hatred digs long shank claws, what will it be like
to be more than that? What will it be to adore the nature
of your killer's affliction?

In whatever epoch of new understanding.
New faiths new religious zeals. The lone saver is knowing exactly
how far to trust what is real. I am tired already
of being so hopelessly right.

Tight Rope

We live in fragments
like speech. Like the fits
of wind, shivering against
the window.

Pieces of meaning, pierced
and strung together. The bright bead
of the poem, the bright bead
of your woman's laughter.

Kenyatta Listening To Mozart

on the back trails, in sun glasses
and warm air blows cocaine from city
to river, and through the brains of
American poets in San Francisco.

                          Separate
              and lose. Spats brush through
                  undergrowths of fiction. Mathematics
              bird, undressed and in sympathy with absolute
                  stillness, and the neutrality of water. (We do not
          write poems in the rainy season.) Light to light,
      the weighted circumstance prowls like animals in the
bush.
          A zoo of consciousness,
                              cries and prowlings

anywhere. Stillness,
                  motion,
                              beings that fly, beings

that swim
exchanging
              in-
                  formation.
                              Choice, and
                              style,
                                      avail

and are beautiful
categories
                  If you go

              for that.

Morning Purpose

Rising gate
with disappearing locks.
Thin tingling wind. Sun engines
picking up their whirr, starlings wheeling
across oil and pulling it into clouds. Turning
as a last measure, to scream. But too far away. The control
is what lifts me. The sky is not open, but curves, in blue sinking tones
to send us back in the deep flesh of our own places. Whip shaped,
to deal with romance.

Averroës' Tempo

Nothing

surprises
me. Except what you can actually
make.

Nothing, then
nothing, for years
or minutes. Till the color seeps in
to the skin, wearing the nerves, as night,
on the outside. And cars go by insensitive,
making french music.
                    Talk
                    among ruins. Dust settling
how many years, to make it plain
as to how far into space my grandfather
leaned.
            Is leaning, as a hacked tree
with news
for hunters.
                Direction,
                        or its multiple reality.
                        (City at the edge/ of flat
                        land.)

                    He leans. (A head)

steering the ship.

After the Ball

The magic dance

of the second ave ladies,

       in the artificial glare
of the world, silver-green curls sparkle
and the ladies' arms jingle
with new Fall pesos, sewn on grim bracelets
the poet's mother-in-law thinks are swell.

       So much for America, let it sweep in grand style
up the avenues of its failure. Let it promenade smartly
beneath the marquees of its despair.
       Bells swing lazily in New Mexico
ghost towns. Where the wind celebrates
afternoon, and leftover haunts stir a little
out of vague instinct,
       hanging their messy sheets
in slow motion against the intrepid dust
or the silence
       which they cannot scare.

DEATH IS NOT AS NATURAL
AS YOU FAGS SEEM TO THINK

I hunt
the black puritan.
         (Half-screamer

in dull tones
of another forest.

Respecter of power. That it transform, and enlarge
Hierarchy crawls over earth (change exalting space
Dried mud to mountain, cape and whip, swirled
Walkers, and riders and flyers.
Language spread into darkness. Be Vowel
                 and value

          Consonant
             and direction.

Rather the lust of the thing
than across to droop at its energies. In melted snows
the leather cracks, and pure men claw at their bodies.
Women laugh delicately, delicately rubbing their thighs.

And the dead king laughs, looking out the hole
in his tomb. Seeing the poor
singing his evil songs.

Legacy

(For Blues People)

In the south, sleeping against
the drugstore, growling under
the trucks and stoves, stumbling
through and over the cluttered eyes
of early mysterious night. Frowning
drunk waving moving a hand or lash.
Dancing kneeling reaching out, letting
a hand rest in shadows. Squatting
to drink or pee. Stretching to climb
pulling themselves onto horses near
where there was sea (the old songs
lead you to believe). Riding out
from this town, to another, where
it is also black. Down a road
where people are asleep. Towards
the moon or the shadows of houses.
Towards the songs' pretended sea.

Mise en Scène: *Newark, 1947*

Green swirling neon snow. Fish shack
closing. A chinaman leans
in the flour, another
recaps empty soda bottles. Fish shack
closing. Four o'clock negroes
sleep or nod or hug
the tables. 26 cents
rung on the register.
A pack of Luckies.
                    The vomiting band leader
looks out wearily
from the phone booth.
He is with a white woman,
whose parents do not know
where she is.

The Success

Among things with souls, find me.

> Picking thru the alphabet
> or leaning out the window. (Lives
> and magic.) Old witch city, the
> lights and roads (floating) up near the tops
> of buildings. Electric names, which are not
> love's. A rolling Eastern distress. Water cutting
> the coast, lulling the mysterious classes.

Murderers humming under the window.

A strutting long headed Negro. Beneath the red silk

of unique social fantasy. Shore invisible under tenements.

The Jew who torments Hitler in Paradise, wiping thick fingers

on a hospital cloth. His fingerprints on the dough, marking it

before baking. Drifting to sleep in Pelham, fucking a female spy.

This man was used against me,
in a dream.

> Broken teeth
> Dirty apron
> Hires a bowery desperado,

> > to pull out the garbage
> > and imagine the whiteness
> > of his wife's withered stomach.

> —

> Ding

> —

> The proportion of Magic
> has seeped so low.

> For the 1st person plural

> America, then,

> > Atlantis,

> > > in blind overdose.

21

The New World

The sun is folding, cars stall and rise
beyond the window. The workmen leave
the street to the bums and painters' wives
pushing their babies home. Those who realize
how fitful and indecent consciousness is
stare solemnly out on the emptying street.
The mourners and soft singers. The liars,
and seekers after ridiculous righteousness. All
my doubles, and friends, whose mistakes cannot
be duplicated by machines, and this is all of our
arrogance. Being broke or broken, dribbling
at the eyes. Wasted lyricists, and men
who have seen their dreams come true, only seconds
after they knew those dreams to be horrible conceits
and plastic fantasies of gesture and extension,
shoulders, hair and tongues distributing misinformation
about the nature of understanding. No one is that simple
or priggish, to be alone out of spite and grown strong
in its practice, mystics in two-pants suits. Our style,
and discipline, controlling the method of knowledge.
Beatniks, like Bohemians, go calmly out of style. And boys
are dying in Mexico, who did not get the word.
The lateness of their fabrication: mark their holes
with filthy needles. The lust of the world. This will not
be news. The simple damning lust,

> float flat magic in low changing
> evenings. Shiver your hands
> in dance. Empty all of me for
> knowing, and will the danger
> of identification,

Let me sit and go blind in my dreaming
and be that dream in purpose and device.

A fantasy of defeat, a strong strong man
older, but no wiser than the defect of love.

HEGEL

Cut out
the insides,
where eyes
bungle their silence, and trains suffer
to be painted
by memory.
                This is turning. As a man
turns. Hardened or reconceived
sometimes the way we wish our lives
would be. "Let me do this
again,
          another way."

   Pushed to the wall
we fall away from each other
in this heresy. Dispute each other's
lives, as history. Or the common speech
of disaster, lacking a face or name, we give it
ours. And are destroyed by the very virtues
of our ignorance.
                I am not saying,
"Let the state fuck
its faggots,"
          only that no fag
          go unfucked, for purely impersonal
          reasons.

   I am trying to understand
the nightmare of economics. On the phone,
through the mails, I am afraid. I scream
for help. I scream
for help. And none comes, has ever
come. No single redeeming hand
has ever been offered,
               even against the excess
               of speech, no single redeeming

    word, has come
     wringing out of flesh
with the imperfect beautiful resolution
that would release me from this heavy contract
of emptiness.
     Either I am wrong
     or "he" is wrong. All right
     I am wrong, but give me someone
     to talk to.

LEADBELLY GIVES AN AUTOGRAPH

Pat your foot
and turn
       the corner. Nat Turner, dying wood
of the church. Our lot
is vacant. Bring the twisted myth
of speech. The boards brown and falling
away. The metal bannisters cheap
and rattly. Clean new Sundays. We thought
it possible to enter
the way of the strongest.

But it is rite that the world's ills
erupt as our own. Right that we take
our own specific look into the shapely
blood of the heart.

             Looking thru trees
the wicker statues blowing softly against
the dusk.
Looking thru dusk
thru dark-
ness. A clearing of stars
and half-soft mud.

The possibilities of music. First
that it does exist. And that we do,
in that scripture of rhythms. The earth,
I mean the soil, as melody. The fit you need,
the throes. To pick it up and cut
away what does not singularly express.

Need.
Motive.
The delay of language.

A strength to be handled by giants.

The possibilities of statement. I am saying, now,
what my father could not remember
to say. What my grandfather
was killed
for believing.
                    Pay me off, savages.
                    Build me an equitable human assertion.

One that looks like a jungle, or one that looks like the cities
of the West.   But I provide the stock. The beasts
and myths.
                    The City's Rise!
                              (And what is history, then? An old deaf lady
                              burned to death
                              in South Carolina.

The Burning General

Smoke seeping from my veins. Loss from
the eyes. Seeing winter throw its wind
around. Hoping for more, than I'll ever
have. Forgetting my projects, and the projected
sense of order, any claim to "sense" must make.
The reason Allen and the others (even freakish
pseudo dada mama) in the money jungle of controlled
pederasty
                  finally bolted. Shut and gone, at the same time.

But can we replace the common exchange of experience with stroking
some skinny girl's penis? Is sense to be lost, all of it, so that
we can walk up Mulberry Street without getting beat up in Italian.

Violence and repression. Silly Nigger hatred for the
silk band of misery. They are right, those farty doctors. Perhaps
it is best to ease into kill-heaven than have no heaven at all.
What do you think, Eddie, out there in Idaho shivering against
the silence, the emptiness of straight up America? What's it look like
there?

Can we ask a man to savor the food of oppression? Even
if it's rich and full of mysterious meaning. Can you establish
(and that word must give my whole game away) and kind of equality?
Can there be such thing forced on the world? That is, that the poor
and their owners appreciate light wherever they are, simply as light.
Why are you so sophisticated? You used to piss and shit in your pants.
Now you walk around *thinking* all the time, as if that sacred act
would rewrite the world in bop talk, giving medals to every limping coon
in creation.

Is there more to it than that? This is the time to ask, even while perfecting
your line. We realize that ends and means should be separated, but who
will do the separating? The evaluating. You want your experience
thought of as valuable. Which is, listen baby, only another kind
of journalistic enterprise. Not worthy of that bumpy madness
crawled up your thighs when the urine dried those sweet lost winters,
and tears were the whole fucking world.

Tone Poem

(for Elvin Jones and Bob Thompson)

A host of loves is the city, and its memory
dead sense traveling (from England) on the sea
for two hundred years. The travelers show up in Japan
to promote peace and prosperity, perhaps a piece
of that nation's ass. Years later, years later,
plays rework the rime of lust. As history, and a cloud
their faces bang invisible notes, wind scribbled leaves
and foam. An eagle hangs above them spinning. Years and travelers
linger among the dead, no reports, gunshots white puffs
deciding the season and the mode of compromise. The general good
has no troops or armor, subtly the books stand closed, except
sàd facts circled for unknown hippies carrying the mail.
I leave it there, for them, full of hope, and hurt. All the poems
are full of it. Shit and hope, and history. Read this line
young colored or white and know I felt the twist of dividing
memory. Blood spoiled in the air, caked and anonymous. Arms opening,
opened last night, we sat up howling and kissing. Men who loved
each other. Will that be understood? That we could, and still
move under cold nights with clenched fists. Swing these losers
by the tail. Got drunk then high, then sick, then quiet. But thinking
(and of you lovely shorties sit in libraries seeking such ideas out).
I'm here now, LeRoi, who tried to say something long for you. Keep it.
Forget me, or what I say, but not the tone, and exit image. No points,
or theories, from now on, just me and mine, when they get me, just
think of me as typing with a drink at my right hand, some women who
love me . . . and the day growing old and sloppy through the window.

Square Business

The faces of Americans
sit open hating each
other. The black ones
hating, though they laugh
and are controlled by
laughter. The white ones
blown up hot inside, their projects
are so profitable . . . sixteen stories
in a sultry town . . . wind bends them
back.

These are boxes
of money. With lids
these winds wont lift.
Winds from foodless mouths.
Steel boxes floating in tears.
In panama hats and floppy pants
in love with happy tasteful God. They
own him. But what do they own? And can it *[handwritten: con blk. be broken]*
be chewed to a liquid?

They own each
other. They own
my mother. They own

29

and own, go on, what else
is theirs?

    Time. Time is.

The pop of the clock, your head
on the block. Or your wife, another
life, to fly us back to historical hate.
They own numbers. But not the strong ones.
One Two Three, they own. And squared. Halved.
Sent for over the telephone. They own
language. Churches. But not the strong ones.
Four Five Six, they own. But not Beaulah
Bapt. or Drifting Image Church Of Christ In
Dreams. Where the old ladies fan themselves
with God. And *things* have *never* existed. But
what else, moving on the cobblestones. What
possibly else, could there be. Can you see?
The light's so bad. Have you paid the bill?
Light and sound, are tied and sealed. Music.
They got that too. Listen to Benny cut his
bread with a mouth piece. You know they got
that. Probably, anything fat. Wind, the spirit
of skinniness. Blow wind! Spirits mumble
in the sun. Skirting the water with
shadowless grace.

Major Bowes' Diary

Flesh chase night, weather booming and dark
hosts of fear pushing the windows even in
plastics land. Meat spells stir the funk
false messages seal the eery light and hook it
to the mind, or a mind, if the identity of pain
must be personal. No one understands masks
and invention, except masqueraders and inventors.
The circle of seeing is that limited, and the thing seen
will look like anything. (With the morning's rise
snow will substitute for music, and the cold pavement
for the scrape of thought. Hands lips moving. Legs
and the bottoms of coats; whipped around in the
midnight wind.

Stars at six, just the two, one dim, the other bright
up near the crescent moon (a lighted mouth static
as consciousness or the soft skin of love. A head
will be filled with someone else's voice. The tips
of the fingers will smell, like that someone.

A comb or womb of what we lay down nightly
in. Sleeping there, outside the ordinary fact
of lie and death. But there, the tired cone
of black love, tilted heavy through head bone
cross and jack to lift the tired soul, crossed staves
of the daring failure's history. Secret cove
of spirit waves of time and loss crack flesh
and dream, he turns there so, cracks simple things
like love. What I, a singer, have for the world
is simple, deadly darkness closing down so hard,
is simple, in defense, a yielded portion of grace.

As people in
my life
are common blankness: hugged in the womb
of the trees or night's whispered geometries. As people,
to consider, Buddha's child, a bearded drunk
considered, in my head of hair the dark is there
and light it lays against my tongue. I feel no thing
but word, picture, conditioning . . . black tomb of possibility . . .
heart, dreams of stinking feet. I feel no single
treachery but what you are having been these few seconds
something like my self.

Cant

The walls are made of rain. The city's walls
of scattered paper, and autographed photos
of Hobbes.

>   (Last remnant of idealness, open
>   ness. Political theorists in brown suede
>   beautiful shoes. Lurch from left to right
>   along the corridors of predicted Grace.
>   Having lost . . . the flags droop, and cling
>   to their wet poles. Booker Washington
>   and Gunga Din, dry lipped, in hell
>   adding their myth to the fortifiers' bulk.)

Knowing the season
as a change of heart.
Black to gold. Thread of reason
whipped against the walls. New winds,
of a complex weather. The naked seek clothes,
the holy, a faster God, to keep the known
in line.

>   Mystery

>   loves company. The popes and witches
caught in paint and metal. "This is a picture
of a beer can. We are no longer
concerned
with light."

>   Make do,
>   with what we have.

>   Tools, like arks.
>   At the mercy of Aristotle,
>   or any missionary/ confusing what we are
for what we could become.

Sleep builds the picture world, widening
rubber fancies spread the walls of any
thing you've ever said. In bed, my head
is lead, and dead. I think of all the
people hearts and songs I need, call them
Flesh, its new but, Flesh, over here,
Flesh. And they drop against my chest.
Women shoes and money. Poems and cars.
Countries words and courage. The assembled
fates and human weights. And if I have none
of them, who am I, or you, if I am reader
you, your eye, are poet?

Tone Row

Open the face of the ignorant, open it, shove splitting images in
cut through the safety lid (dwindled standing garbage saturday dying).
Old cut the love we feel moving a hill vaunts its sky a long factory
holding, the city and my life a useless box of noise, for poets imagining
they are Shakespeare's hardon, or the hairless prince whose dick he sucked.
Literature, then, is feeling, and never quiet gasps of befuddlement
at the world. "Bird is *symbol*," an old fart with a typewriter hoping his hand
wont shake the poem away. Lead him out a stuttering hero, garland and
warm his two huge feet. Give 'im a dime, if he needs it. Send him eating
into the strophe yard huge like empty Dachau, yellow flowers thru old jew
bones. He wanders peeing in imaginary books. His soul is illiterate
the fingers of his nightmare climb the walls of jails and scream at trains.
He sits and wonders where the girl who dragged his feeling sideways saturdays
sun slanting on new hats under the marquees of adolescence, the throb
of possible lovers, young boys pray their futures in, the bathroom door
stays locked.

    Old sheepish snoring (holding) time. It beats
    and crosses ankles, church dance lie and way
    they moved those old time days. Moved, and still
    there, are simple things, a pinstriped coat and
    painty pants. Singing on a guitar, made up roads
    and loves. Old man. Older than shape, his fingers
    pull the music out.

Loku

Hold me she
told me I
did.

On Out

Wheel music
moon across windows

Feeling, like the world, in
so many places. (Train roars thru
dead dark. Lights ringing
on fences, air, night, slide
on the outside, and I ride
pinned together in the fast light.

History As Process

1.

*The evaluation of the mysteries by the sons of all
experience.* All suffering, if we call the light a thing
all men should know. Or find. Where ever, in the dark folds
of the next second, there is some diminishing beauty we might one day
understand, and scream to, in some wild fit of acknowledged Godliness.

Reality, is what it is. This suffering truth
advertised in all men's loveliest histories.

The thing, There As Speed, is God, as mingling
possibility. The force. As simple future, what

the freaky gipsies rolled through Europe
on.

(The soul.)

2.

What can I do to myself? Bones
and dusty skin. Heavy eyes twisted
between the adequate thighs of all
humanity (a little h), strumming my head
for a living. Bankrupt utopia sez tell me
no utopias. I will not listen. (Except the raw wind
makes the hero's eyes close, and the tears that come out
are real.)

DAVID COPPERHEAD

On the stairs, in the house, on a street
in the world. Thought and wind, running.
Yellow clocks, Black wizards,
appear, and disappear, the woman I'm thinking
about is so beautiful. She controls my dreams,
and my reality. No choice, stirs a blue midnight
wind windy like cool brushes stuttering. The roof
is a stage, here all things go on. Go on.

(Booted twice, missed on the squeeze
and my arm shot up. A knot now, where
the high is wasted, and the head
only a little twittered, from
small heart, and lack of skill.)

Heart of a small dog, near water
in the summer. Winter, ice, and
slowness of the iron trees. What
have people to do with the world.
Whatever you think, the opposite
could also be. And any wavelength
in between.

(Now to consider, whether to go
again. I still need that feeling.
And sit robbed, my head twists,
from that lack. Always, and never,
a rationalist. But gut thought
rubbing all surfaces. Knife gripped hard
in the hand. Let fire break out
and stop us. Forget pink cardboard
suns. Gold halos. Slow run of water.
Some women are around. They walk and
never even miss us. He flies down
from the stage. The moon is gone.)

Feeling predicts
intelligence. The boats, pointing
West.

The Visit

What I never wanted, came back
for me to love it. (Above the sirens
and bogus magic of the laughably damned) Came back,
in a new way, into new heart . . . old things considered
there light struck me, social songs, racial songs,
and love, like a versified cliché, came down on me
hard, in its casual way. Tell me what it looked like.
And me, who did I resemble? Mute shadow of perfection.
Blessed and blessed, seeing, smelling, strength alert
in my weakest parts.

She is a thing of suffering. Yellow girl. Gone
in the subways, my heart
pounding above the train

GATSBY'S THEORY OF AESTHETICS

Verse, as a form, is artificial. Poetry is not a form, but rather a result. Whatever the matter, its meaning, if precise enough in its information (and direction) of the world, is poetic. The poetic is the value of poetry, and any concatenation of elements is sufficient to induce the poetic. What you see is as valuable as what you do not. But it is not as meaningful (to you). Poetry aims at difficult meanings. Meanings not already catered to. Poetry aims at reviving, say, a sense of meaning, or meaning's possibility and ubiquitousness.

Identification can be one term of that possibility. That is, showing a thing with its meaning apparent through the act of that showing. Interpretation can be another term. That is, supporting a meaning, with one's own life. That is, under, standing. And using that position as a map, or dictionary. Depending on whether you move or sit.

I write poetry only to enlist the poetic consistently as apt description of my life. I write poetry only in order to feel, and that, finally, sensually, all the terms of my life. I write poetry to investigate my self, and my meaning and meanings.

But also to invest the world with a clearer understanding of it self, but only by virtue of my having brought some clearer understanding of my self into it. I wrote in a poem once, "Feeling predicts intelligence."

But it is possible to feel with any part of our consciousness. Whatever part of us does register: whatever. The head feels. The heart feels. The penis feels. The penis is also, because it is able to feel, conscious, and has intelligence of its own. No one can deny that intelligence, or at least no one should try. The point of life is that it is arbitrary, except in its basest forms. Arbitrariness, or self imposed meaning, is the only thing worth living for. It is the only thing that permits us to live.

The only time I am conscious of my limitations is when I am writing. The rest of the time, there is no standard, at all reasonable, for judging, in fact, what limitations are.

Year of the Buffalo
1964

Lately

Heart claws
out into the street. Weak evil eyes
follow its progress in cabs (with crabs)
the sky like a drying sore, that progress, swift,
motherless, away from the normal fact of adventure
and response. Away from women, heart, rushing
under cool night air.

         (If I were there
         her soft brown
         hair, for eating,
         pulling, smothering
         life from in you, if I
         were really, there.)

               Magic of lust
              is emotional thrift
                sudden movement, flying heart
              quiet auctioned in the blood
           dirty veins throw error to the head.

       Heart trackers lean in heart's wind
       The mouths of their cars hang open
       Where's heart going . . . bending tall
       and natural things, to simple human
       failure, feeling, open a window,
       or something.

       Up third street speeds/

              and finally
              dis
              appears.

              Old hard
              red thing

              I'll miss
              you

All's Well

(For E. R. & M. B.)

African in the Bush of the Hatreds. One gone.

An old time love withered, in seeing, off and on
in a thing like rain (the wetness in your head, and
all the stampeding, fear, hacked open skulls grinning
sensing your loss, the words floating just beyond your
fingers (invisible antennae

Just drew a blank, dope nod
corrupting what's left, and that nothing
confusion of blankness, the hatred when I wake
silence for motives, she, woman I am with, is
silent, as the dream of some other woman, never
existed, tho she be of flesh and red sperm spinning
through her veins. This woman came when I stuck her
iron insect screams holes. Blood flew up into the
dropper, we sent it back in her. Eyes rolled up,
lap quivered, lip shook. The next time she
got depressed going cross town. She held me so.
Not understanding the buildings stopped, and sky
hung above them just the same

The Bronze Buckaroo

for Herb Jeffries

Soft night comes back
with its clangs and dreams. Back
in through the base
of the hairy skull. The heavy pictures, unavailable
solaces, emptying their churchy magic
out. Golden girls, and thin black ones
patrol the dreamer's meat. Things
shovel themselves, from where they always are. Spinning, a
moment's indecision, past the vision of stealth and silence
Byron thought the night could be. Death blow Eliot silence, dwindling
away, in the 20th century. Poet clocks crouched in their Americas.
Dreaming of poems, only the cold sky could bring. Not room poems, or
fireplace poems, or the great washed poetry of our dizzy middleclass.
But something creeps and grabs them, rapes them on the pavement. The Screams
are not essays, rich blonde poetess from the mysteries of Kipling's harmon
nica! Not guileful treatises of waste and desire, stuck somewhere
nursing her tilted beauty, like some old fashion whore, embarrassed
by God, or his diseases. The funny heart blows smoke, in the winter
and gives us all the earth we need. In summer, it sweats, and remembers.
Half way up the hill the mutineers stand, and seek their comrades out.
I am half way up, and standing.

Target Study

1963–1965

Numbers, Letters

If you're not home, where
are you? Where'd you go? What
were you doing when gone? When
you come back, better make it good.
What was you doing down there, freakin' off
with white women, hangin' out
with Queens, say it straight to be
understood straight, put it flat and real
in the street where the sun comes and the
moon comes and the cold wind in winter
waters your eyes. Say what you mean, dig
it out put it down, and be strong
about it.

I cant say who I am
unless you agree I'm real

I cant be anything I'm not
Except these words pretend
to life not yet explained,
so here's some feeling for you
see how you like it, what it
reveals, and that's me.

Unless you agree I'm real
that I can feel
whatever beats hardest
at our black souls

I am real, and I can't say who
I am. Ask me if I know, I'll say
yes, I might say no. Still, ask.

I'm Everett LeRoi Jones, 30 yrs old.
A black nigger in the universe. A long breath singer,
wouldbe dancer, strong from years of fantasy
and study. All this time then, for what's happening
now. All that spilling of white ether, clocks in ghostheads
lips drying and rewet, eyes opening and shut, mouths churning.

47

I am a meditative man. And when I say something it's all of me
saying, and all the things that make me, have formed me, colored me
this brilliant reddish night. I will say nothing that I feel is
lie, or unproven by the same ghostclocks, by the same riders
always move so fast with the word slung over their backs or
in saddlebags, charging down Chinese roads. I carry some words,
some feeling, some life in me. My heart is large as my mind
this is a messenger calling, over here, over here, open your eyes
and your ears and your souls; today is the history we must learn
to desire. There is no guilt in love

YOUNG SOUL

First, feel, then feel, then
read, or read, then feel, then
fall, or stand, where you
already are. Think
of your self, and the other
selves . . . think
of your parents, your mothers
and sisters, your bentslick
father, then feel, or
fall, on your knees
if nothing else will move you,

> then read
> and look deeply
> into all matters
> come close to you
> city boys—
> country men
>
> Make some muscle
> in your head, but
> use the muscle
> in yr heart

Confirmation

The blood in me, assumes a beautiful shape, it assumes
that I can write, and that I am the great mind of my own
soul, in a fit of fall flashing bells, the great booms
and machines that make the world worth exploding and re-
building, for whatever we agree on is most honorable.

There is no struggle to speak if you want to.
There is no slowness or stupidity we must bear.
There is perfection! There is grace! There are
all those things they talked about . . . but different!
Jesus Christ, how different! How much bullshit did they
put into our way, how much ugliness we canonized, dazed
and dazzing in
The Music is so strong,
it smashes through the boards. It questions
the beat of my mind, where the soul beats against the iron badges
of a cage. How hateful can be anything. How it can turn you, resurrect your errors as if the mind laughed at what it hated to use, and
used the fingers of your consciousness to dazzle yourself with madness.

We can be used by everything. We are not in danger of being wrong.
Only stupid, in the quiet despotic night. Oh, how the freaks of this
adventure sadden, the old ladies walking by scared and scaring, not
even caring that the world is falling apart, and even the intellectuals
will be killed. Oh, Christ you don't understand. I don't understand
what the problem has to do with this woman's lips, or that woman's
understanding of why is the world is finally so ugly, even though
you're right. The world is the most perfect thing in the soul. The world
is a soul, and we are souls if we remember the murmurs of the spirit.

Witches and Devils

Harder blood-blizzards. Rain avalanches. A whining
like voices, remembering their memories, turning turned
around. Almighty shit stealer in the automobile flash of world ecstasy.
(This is what they don't want to give us. Ecstasy. Simple pussy. Betrayers
of their kind, West Man, betrayers of laughter and ease, West Men, white
guys, brujo explosions could free you,
a sweet eye-rich cop could stumble head long
down

Dirk—The undressed, can sail. (*Walking out through the windows, shinnying
          out to the edge of the flagpole*) Looks like a dick, to me!
Johnnie May—(*Answering, with her little silver bell voice . . . from 35 stories
          down*) The spectacle is a groove. Is everybody here this short?

Could there be mountains. (There could be soap
sinking in soapy water. There could be nod hookey, a famous form
of latent christianity.

          His arm rose like something was scrambling
               under his skin.

                    My arm rose, I keep in a warm pool
                         of breath.

We are winter organs. Steel insects
fill us with madness.

Friday

And so we leave. Hurrying. The bags packed,
minds in halfzoom position. One kit I carry,
contents: 3 knives, a revolver, 1½ ounces of
bush. Then get in
the wind.

All ready. All
right. Clinks jingles cries
through doors and windows
where the sun follows, in its quick breath,
matching our own I am rising. The air is still.
Heaven comics on the roof. My room sir william
butler will you answer the door of attention. To be
concerned, with ourselves, and the not knowing
even as the wind marauds, and the Gods change
faces.

When you are dead Good. And let the crying cease. Baroomed off a ship of the second measure. The measure of the rhythm, hear me, stretching past Your eyes.

Oh simple weak minded gods,
who walk the simple streets of circumstances. Who lie
to people, to animals, to doors and excellent rugs. Oh power
full juggernauts whose most powerful image is the hairy cock
sucker of art. (Uncle Sam is a queer whose ass hangs open with
the brown odor of his heroes' delight. Pimps whose mothers ate
vermin from the chauffeur's piles, and giggled like the sweet babies of
innocent adventure.) A fart over the world demanding the power of our
lives.

Oh, later, later for them. Let them go out of our lives.
Let them kill themselves in their cars, or debowel themselves
with their useless energies.

Even softer, come on, sit down now,
relent. The window is open. Soft cars rise and
fall. Your mind and eyes are open. You are strong. Leave
them Leave
them

Here He Comes Again

Dark crowds in my face, my lips
get big and important my nose
is suddenly strange mixture of
temperament and temperature. All
the black sealed in me flies to
the surface, and beneath it, more
of the same. Like a hard deep rock
I had to tell a hooknosed lady panting
at my fly, I didn't care whether she died
I had my own history of deaths and submission

I don't love you

Whatever you've given me, whiteface glass
to look through, to find another there, another
what motherfucker? another bread tree mad at its
sacredness, and the law of some dingaling god, cold
as ice cucumbers, for the shouters and the wigglers,
and what was the world to the words of slick nigger fathers,
too depressed to explain why they could not appear to be men.

The bread fool. The don'ts of this white hell. The crashed eyes
of dead friends, stanind at the bar, eyes focused on actual ugliness.

I don't love you. Who is to say what that will mean. I don't
love you, expressed the train, moves, and uptown days later
we look up and breathe much easier

I don't love you

Sky King

The touch of God like
structure   wetsmells
count her mouth lies—
piling material. Tension
of moving clouds, if you fly
you know the turbulence

Travel Agent

Their hearts are cities and away from them
they are old witches, dead touching, weak wind
from the sea. They want to go home. And they look, always,
in that direction. Though there is no direction, but out.
And the things floating in fat foolishness, plants and statements.
Sick events. Make a wall of impossible logic. Heads full of distance
and dishonest passion. Make a wall, a wall, a high wall of strain.
We left our remarkable loving, but we wont do that
again.

Correction

Lay all of it open. The black phrase, the face, the way
down through the wet pictures, sea walls, down on sightings
nothing is so calm that it can be exact, and recorded, my shadow
sliding on the wall, the outside time breeze dragging lost women
through the evening, and the dead chirping of insects, hidden pressures
born this one second, as if I wept for my memory, a lost young beautiful
boy. As if those times were still to come, and my face had not been
opened.

It could be a new strength, a cunning like the common night. A seeing
as if in hurtled bliss, the freckles sunshine woodair smells and
radio language purring utopias of emotion. God must smile, and drag
through the playground smiling, seeing that people do not recognize him
nor does he recognize himself, being skinny and timid, and finally nasty.

What is a road you can tell about? The findings, small letters, a light,
the way of misunderstanding smoke rising from a tub, and the bather blue
tortured, the smile of a madman lighting up the backyard useless sandbox.

Haul ass . . . this is a thing you can tell them. If somebody will let you be
Seven foot and husky, if somebody will let you be, a tender singing thing.

The penalty for piracy

Eyes come back. See something. Over there's
a sad man, with his world, blown, so he must
build another, or whatever other, is most beautiful.
In a corner, another sad man. He will not weep. The
penalty for piracy
"is not dripped thru
  a cloth," nor does it come down
like an avalanche of everything. It is
The Penalty
and hangs with you
in that cold breeze
while your hair congeals
and your mouth turns a hideous
pout.

The Poisoned God

What we see in the persons of our feeling
is driven there. The stones drying in the cellar
memory's flowers   above the older buildings   cries
and lost stealths.   Singing   religions   fall away
nights the stars are straightened.

Tonight a long way ago.   Mary's long body
reflecting the odor of her mind   history and jingles
movie-love, where the end's your own beginning.   And light
is no single meaning.   Like the strain of being alone
when you're kindest.   Watching workmen ignore the sun.

Wind crissed, twisting the bird's crusts   near sparkling windows
and a few ideas.

Believe in nothing   except the nothings of your walking.
Killer typographies   meekly dumped in the banks of your thinking.
        (Birds eat, then fly away,
to use something else   like phones, or dead clothes swinging
underwater. With the fish   and searched for merchant ships.

With the idea of listening   with your ears, and fingers
stretching into the water.   Tasting the silence so it crushes
your wanting. Hacked and older   so that sense leaves
and a lie replaces it

Dada Zodji

Ships crowd west, in long lines
floating culture in. New ports and
stalls, designed by disease and money.
The honeyed genius hoists a flag. Storm
warning, of nationalism and misguided
archaeology. Manning steel ships to kill
their brothers. Along both coasts of gold.

Twist is a bird
whose wings are wet
from eating on the fly. (Ship lanes
in sraight lines. For harmony and
the stacked deck of power's measure.
"Millions killed themselves,"

         in the dark. Jumping

off buildings and boats
complex geography of motives. Red dot
to red dot, from waters marked in light blue
along the coast. But their histories are blurred.
Misread for effect. Booms that shattered the ears
of schoolboys too young to see in the dark.

         (Which,
         they say,

  was their own flesh

  And

     now poleaxed to the vacant cement
     they want an herb to bring them back.
     Restore their flesh and noise (for their fathers
     who vanished into elevators loosening
     their ties. Vowing not to drink or swear
     until the man would let them see God. (A white man
     with
       a dueling scar.

I want
to see God. If you know
him. Biblically, have
fucked him. And left him wanting,
in a continuous history of defeat. Screaming, then,
in a fog of meanings settling on the rotting crop.

When I was coolest
they said I limped. Was lame,
and had no future past memory.

                    Restore me, was a song
                    I made. Let me drink
                    of the high getter. Let me
                    seriously lose my mind.

Limping
across an ocean. With no tongue
to give my children their names.

Claiming the useless parts of vegetables, and a music
too close to hysteria.

                  A coloring device. Universe of tones.
                  Claim now, an old fly, little letter God
              who has gone to bed wth no one
                for the last 300 years.

Will They Cry When You're Gone, You Bet

You leave dead friends in
a desert. But they've deserted
you, and them-
selves, and are leaving
themselves,
in the foot paths
of madmen and saints
enough sense to get away
from the dryness and uselessness
of such relaxation, dying in the dry
light, sand packed in their mouths
eyes burning, white women serenade them
in mystic deviousness, which is another
way of saying they're seeing things, which
are not really there, except for them,
never to find an oasis, even bitter water
which we get used to, is better than
white drifting fairies, muses, singing
to us, in calm tones, about how it is better to die
etcetera, than go off from them, how it is better to
lie in the cruel sun with your eyes turning to dunes
than leave them alone in that white heat,

What am I offered

Six foot tall, once president
united states, small letters for
10 years, drawls, what they used
to call, Texas . . . cow-boy . . . talk,
scrawls, rolls, lies, all washed away
smoke rising over the moon, still red,
blood of the century twisting long drops
hung down through space,

                can work as hustler
                cracklicker, or brilliant god
                (in a reconstructed devil world.

                Strong beliefs, Hairless,
                Very very white.

Cold Term II

We make crazy lullabies
heartpushing, wailing in the innards
shit thrown across the blue heavens
spelling constant cool despair. Why
am I like this Knowing the world
so well yet open to its dumbest
disorders? I wanted a black woman.
And had one. She went away. I drove her
away, and had nothing left
but the endless mosquito babble
of my weakness. The Dancing Crimes
so full of wisdom we overlook the pure shit
involved. A landscape
made of
shit. A world.

Sad Cowboy

All the world, is hatred
and I think I am love, or where are you fool
to think you're different from some body,
you've felt pain, your mind has opend as meat
and sweat. The place, is the final determination.
What is your place in the order of your feelings?
As the runner for your nation, focused on their needs,
what can you say or dream or float wild copper love in place of,
what you had, which was white and soft, and the vision of the farm
boy, standing in his shit. Replacing the man, and defining his demise.
But that crap is finished. I move with the rest, as strong as they,
knowing my own mind to be the unneeded rationale, the kindly explanation

Blue Whitie

Strange corpses the ones who
still talk. Here is one now.
Tell us, sir, why are you so
full of shit? Now, come on, Man, don't be afraid,
speak right up into the microphone.

Ration

Banks must be robbed,
the guards bound and gagged.

The money must be taken
and used to buy weapons.

Communications systems
must be seized, or subverted.

The machines must be turned
off.

Smoke plenty of bush
before and after work,

or during the holdup
when the guards are iced.

Premises Not Quite Condemned

An altered man
in the sea of a city
in his head he's a dreamer
white women and cars, the rotting artifacts
of lost uncivilizations. His hair is long,
his face round, sometimes soft voice smiles
toward the seat of desire.

What is the prediction
of the peoples? What is their pleasure?
Will they let him live who has sinned
for his strength through the garbage
of his ways? Will they let him breathe
in the maze he has created, riding
on his shoulders through the gale
of his invective. The children
of his thinking, are stronger
than he is, will they pity or
respect, the old old infant.

Here's the drum that is his head
and the scale that is his logic

Rolled on the streets of the niggers.

Call him down
Make him talk

And an explanation start.

Let the old men have it
Let the punks take it

And let the strong men who he loves use him and his ways
for the strength of the peoples
and the strength of the logic

and his rest will be never, for the talk
he will inspire

Let him live, when he dies
and give birth to
brightness

A Poem for Oswald Spengler

Clouds hit the delicately balanced mountains, the walkers
already up, or scaling, through the mist, advertised
in their brains as danger, neon, blink down way off right
nit houses collect, and green. Tomorrow mixmatch rangers
will try to flush us. And then go back, having been summoned
to the white house, to suck the president's dick. We have such
delays in the war, and snares of emotion. Now weird birds
smell our breakfast, and the women in the group shoo them
with washrags.

Red Eye

(for Calvin Hernton and Ishmael Reed)

The corrupt madness of the individual. You cannot live
alone. You are in the world. World, fuck them. World rise
and twist like you do, night madness in rain as heavy as stones.
Alabama gypsy talk, for peeling lips. Look in your mother's head,
if you really want to know everything. Your sister's locked up
pussy. Invasion of the idea syndrome like hand clapping winter in.
Winter will make you move. Or you will freeze in Russia and
never live to see Napoleon as conceived by Marlon Brando.
We are at the point where death is too good for us. We are
in love with the virtue of evil. This communication. Rapping
on wet meat windows, they spin in your head, if I kill you
will not even have chance to hate me

Storage

(after L. McL.)

Joyce Cadoo
27 St. Marks Place
AL4–1407

↑

She Know
  Rich People

Lowdown

We are in the era of imminent brake failure, breakdown
Country boys make believe they are emerging from pyramid crypts.
I talked to a man the other day, and he didn't want to say anthing.
He just drove his train, dreaming of Columbia. Subway hollering roach children
to stretch the conductor out. Copper wire stretched to its maximum tolerance,
copper children loll in their chains dreaming of the chinese bomb. Now we
got the rhythm, and the first threat to White Eye since 1000 (Wogs slowed at
Tours, and the time got different. Era of The Man, now in decline, even
mailmen grow murderous offspring who sightsee in manhattan only to peep
closeup on suicide. The Wanderers. Time/Space syndrome, movement in space
as primitive as that is, as primitive as pimples in cold caves of Europe.
Red sores on their lips imagine what these men sought for the world. What
they wanted to give. For these long centuries. Their idealism was toejam.
Smeared on jewchrist, that's hunkie bread, turned green in the mold of
their shaky enterprises. Even paper not backed by gold. Last shot of three
different movies shows the money blown skyhigh to god, and other forces

A Western Lady

The sick tightening. Brain damage movie
of forbidden flesh, laying in the shadows
breathing without purpose, meat stacked
in terrible silence, her mother wept
to think of that meat, her father, paced
and said the star spangled banner into
his brain damage soup. These were windows
we looked through. The brother died in a
guitar school, stringing guitars and praying
for a piece. And it was his own movie star
slipping green panties over high heels. Hence
his pimples, and the bunching of his waistband.
No one is expected to be rich *and* smart. Hence
planes go down from 30,000, full of screaming
materialists, whose mothers stunted them
hanging around election machines. It was the metal clack
that did it. A flag lobotomy, which has the victims
wallowing on warehouse floors, whistling popular Bach.
I suffer with these announcers. Butter and egg men,
whose promise rolled with the big ice, them's pre-
historic times.

Corregidor

Hard bursts (heart, a word before, hard heart
bursts, Sweetheart it's early in our lives, in our
freakish feel of strength. Don't give it away, or
ourselves. The man's dead, he died tryin'a fly, oh baby
you knew you cdn't make it, but don't say nothin
about me.

I'd rather ride than stay here crying. I'd rather
get weakkneed explaining my actions like sweetwilly the
crybaby. I'd rather sit in the playground, with one finger
curled in the fence. Summer or winter we remember ourselves
and forget the click of the logic. Answers seem dull

In the darkness our motives are easy, our flesh is our weapon
and we kill each other in a fast shuffle dreams drying against
the windows. You never loved me, how could you cry them sham chanties,
so desperate is the nature of this white woman that she will confuse
what she is for what she wants, and confuse me with Barney Google or Santa
Claus or John Apple nodding in his clothes.

76

Third Avenue, Early Winter

As if the trucks were
slaves,
    and slobbered over their chains.

We are not afraid of anything
What we are afraid of is anything
The score is the hide and dull greens
of your shelter. Shadows hat on the
house. A blue black like no night
like no dream of magic

(At the corner
shining beneath the light
The Oldest Living Jewishamerican fairy
in captivity

Hands

Sun makes shadow following a hung man's stick.
It drags, his back curled shades, string
of dribble glistening in same light. "Help me
buy a seeing eye . . ." sign of a dead picket,
hung, strung, right across the earth to somebody's
pocket. Junkies move on a long string. Slobber blood
from their noses, crumbling in front of Carnegie
Why don't you give that man your money? Why doncha'
huh? It was an inside curve ball, struck him out,
and he looked up at the crowd hoping his mother
had a cinder in her eye. But she was hung on a string
with this lewd nigger junkie, jiggling in the cold.
She didn't know what got into her. It'll be a rough job
for ballistics.

You'd be strange too
if you lived in a nation
of ashamed homosexuals. Now that Europe
has turned queer, and the ballplayers (got
that) pat each other in front of everybody.
And the president goes for dogs, and the dogs
wear Chanel, and own radio stations, and mispronounce
the spiritual bleeding. We are moving through the streets
five oclock dead tired dreaming of dying white men. We
flex our trigger fingers on 14th street dreaming of dying
white men. We look up at the flag cold wednesday, at center,
in october, my birth feeling, turns the season, new now can something
ram through your veins, nodding under god, and still dreamed
of dying white men. It rained, it stopped, he fucked and came.
He walked near supermen whose grandmothers lived in Dublin. He
puts small bits of herb in the end of a cigarette, thinking of
amazing language, but move and stop were dream and core of who
he moved and said he loved tho he this tall nothing rain god
had larger flights, these dreams psychiatrist sucking around
rich pussy would be God's function in newtown, utopia, euphoria,
under closed lids of the corners, now cold dead in the whitehouse.
These dreams, go back to the cold caves of Europe, the horses snorting
cold air and cocaine snow, they rise and ride to kill the beautiful Moors.
Slung on a horse (a dime a day, no show, blow the whole load) fast motherfucker, still dreaming . . . RISE GOD FROM SLUM FACTORY
                                        SUCKER OF RHYTHM
                                                            LORD

79

(in sneakers he moves so quiet
with a big razor he will beatify
What bright hand struck at Hiroshima?
To be in love so long, and stare at
the water, without yourself, or a
single beautiful white woman. Now
he will move, still faster . . . love . . .
love, where are you, I want you,
BLACK MAN DREAMING OF MURDER
GET THE SHIT AND MEET ME
SOMEPLACE,

     dreams
     the word in happy-talk (thats
     german psych-floogie for hard
     on,

       the projected singings
       name stars fly past them
       to where we still rule.
       The assembled laughed, in
       white hat and red suspenders.
       "You dumb farmer," I began

all of the wordless music, all of the eyeless meanings

        all of us who are left
        alone too much.

          This poem now has said
          what it means, left off
          life gone seconds ago

Western Front

My intentions are colors, I'm filled with
color, every tint you think of lends to mine
my mind is full of color, hard muscle streaks,
or soft glow round exactness registration. All earth
heaven things, hell things, in colors circulate
a wild blood train, turns litmus like a bible coat,
describes music falling flying, my criminal darkness,
static fingers, call it art, high above the streetwalkers
high above real meaning, floaters prop themselves in pillows
letting soft blondes lick them into serenity. Poems are made
by fools like Allen Ginsberg, who loves God, and went to India
only to see God, finding him walking barefoot in the street,
blood sickness and hysteria, yet only God touched this poet,
who has no use for the world. But only God, who is sole dope
manufacturer of the universe, and is responsible for ease
and logic. Only God, the baldhead faggot, is clearly responsible,
not, for definite, no cats we know.

Alone and Centered:

I went out in the cold, stood around, not knowing
which way,
was mine,
I stood out in the cold, the clear wind blinding me
not understanding
or not wanting to understand
the strength
of my mind.
Alone and centered, in the black wind, or the wind from bodies
whirling devils
painting jews
cunt teasers
my own brothers
in the weight of the gift of balance
Libra, in a strong wind able to rock just slightly
from side to side, it's why I like to fuck
so much, the motion is my own spirit, though
I get cold like ice sidewalk a few seconds
after the juice leaves, and want only to
plunder in my images. Heat from a different flame.

Where is the romantic life?

There's cold slush in the streets, two letters
from simple minded white "theatregoers," on the desk,
Little Anthony on his plastic side, waiting for his play,
Miles of work, and music stumbling beside me. I want anything
you got, having nothing, myself, I want what I want, what I think
I want
I want
what you have, having nothing, myself,
I want
what you are, being nothing, myself,
I want always to be
where I am, and feel
good about it. Some
nerve.

20th-Century Fox

Dynamite black girl
fucking in the halls
skirt pulled up
climbing cross the walls

Dynamite black girl
in her dreams, in her motions, in her pull down hat,
sticks out her lip
asks me where I'm at

Dynamite black girl
outside the shaky mansions of whiteladies
she wears no gown dragging bonebodies of the starving,
nor is she grooved to be talked to by artistic chalksissyghosts

Dynamite black girl,
walks in the snow
meets me in the city
walks with me
stares at me
touches me
talks and talks
to me
kisses me
makes love,
            we said awhile back
            Dynamite black girl
            swingin' in the halls
            the world cant beat you
            and my slaps are love

Poem

For their clean bodies, and malcolm's eyes
I walk the streets confused and half sick
with despair at what I must do, yet the doing
as it's finally possible, drags me on. The way out
feeling inside where I reach, the stones and lights
of new town, new black, new strength, new wealth,
all come down, and back, and the length, of my
health.
My world.
There's not a feeling or fissure sailing
to the stars. Not a strong lady dancing
on the heads of fat white guys, who lick
their bony lips or suck their grey fat teeth.
You see the men who die of cancer and heart trouble.
You see their niggers, fat men with freckles whose minds
are like endless garbage cans, full of blue rats and lies
and the stale vomit of dead Greeks. What is the soul to do
but expand. In the circle of being, the cycle of spirit, the closeness
of love when it's us who are loved, and made huge by some lady
we feel in our speech, or the image of home, in the valley of the blind,
we give them eyes, who we lost, where they drive the suitcases of
glassmenagerie widows, like it's illinois freaks popping their fingers
to Patti Page (who is for future reference, a dumb bitch), if the world
was the man or the god or the song of some specific dier, what more
could you say about it? Who are you walking through the night, where
is this night, my heart expands in the darkness, and sings, if it can,

We say, you will never
understand yourself as an object.
You don't know how you got here,
where you're going, so what's all this bullshit
philosophy

Reading and Weeping

Lust hearts stalk nights
dreaming heroes of them
selves, lust
hearts, screaming
soul, soul, soul, soul,
without the least
memory
of what a soul is
like, they stalk
nights dreaming
reality is their
dying flesh, predicting
the deaths of everyone
but themselves, who are
already dead, and fixed
to their deadness even
in warm spring wind.

Do not cross lust
hearts, they mean
to be killers, and
it is no matter that
you be black or sterilely
pale, they will kill you
if you cross them, if you
dare to speak of a breathing
world, they will menace you if
you are stronger than they are,
they will try to bring you down,
beware the lust hearts, you see them
slinking through the world certain of
their beauty, but look at them, and make them
look at themselves, it is a horrible experience.

Air

I am lost in hot fits
of myself
trying
to get
out. Lost
because
I am kinder
to myself
than I
need
Softer
w/ others
than is good
for them.

Taller
than
most/
Stronger
What is it
about me
that
frightens me
loses
me
tosses me helplessly
in
the air.

Oh love
Songs
dont leave
w/o me
that you
are the weakness
of my simplicity

Are feeling
& want
All need
& romance
I wd do anything
to be loved
& this
is a stupid
mistake.

Poem for Religious Fanatics

There is a sickness to the black man
living in white town. Either he is white
or he hates white, but even in hating, he
reflects, the dead image of his surrounding.
His moon is saw dust marble. His walk is long
and fast, because he doesn't want the reality
of his impotence to sting, instead he will sting
you, before you ask him to look deeply into any reflector
and see himself eating gravel and dust, and old wood hearts.
There is a sickness to the black man in white town, because
he begins to believe he can beat everybody's ass, and he can,
down there, where each man is an island, and the heaviest bomber,
throwing down tnt can establish some conditional manhood in the land
of the dead, in the country of the blind. A one-eyed man, with rotting
palms, king of the tribes of the lost and the dead.

          But we have gone away
          from you, one-eyed man, cannibal,
          o slickest weapon of the romes
          we have left you, to come back
          to ourselves. We have gone away from
          the dead forests of your allergic kingdom
          away from your evil fear of women, away from
          your heavy screamings of anti-fact, and left you
          with your brothers, who are no kin to you at all.

89

Precise Techniques.
No immature bullshitting.
No threatening of people's lifes for bullshit objectives.
No more being a quick Nigger Hero.
The Tony Curtis of the Black Plague.
Because all that is white, no matter your bald
stares out on children playing on the sidewalk,
and pretend you would rule them with a selfish complex.
There is no dream of Man that haunts him such as Freedom!
Dispossessed spirits feeding on soulmeat. Because they do not know enough
to hate the white man. Or deal him those fancy death blows. God
is not a nigger with a beard. Nor
is he not. Question principles not
excitement. And what you laugh at will be hip
anyway

Cold Term

All the things. The objects.
Cold freeze of the park, while
passing. People there. White inside
outside on horses trotting ignorantly
There is so much pain for our blackness
so much beauty there, if we think to what
our beautiful selves would make
of the world, steaming turning blackouts
over cold georgia, the spirits hover
waiting for the world to arrive at ecstasy.
Why cant we love each other and be beautiful?
Why do the beautiful corner each other and spit
poison? Why do the beautiful not hangout together
and learn to do away with evil? Why are the beautiful
not living together and feeling each other's trials?
Why are the beautiful not walking with their arms around
each other laughing softly at the soft laughter of black beauty?
Why are the beautiful dreading each other, and hiding from
each other? Why are the beautiful sick and divided
like myself?

Jitterbugs

The imperfection of the world
is a burden, if you know it, think
about it, at all. Look up in the sky
wishing you were free, placed so terribly
in time, mind out among new stars, working
propositions, and not this planet where you
cant go anywhere without an awareness of the hurt
the white man has put on the people. Any people. You
cant escape, there's no where to go. They have made
this star unsafe, and this age, primitive, though yr mind
is somewhere else, your ass aint.

Word from the Right Wing

President Johnson
is a mass murderer,
and his mother,
was a mass murderer,
and his wife
is wierd looking, a special breed
of hawkbill cracker
and his grandmother's
wierd dumb and dead
turning in the red earth
sick as dry blown soil
and he probably steals
hates magic
and has no use
for change, tho changing, and changed
the weather plays its gambling
tune. His mother is a dead blue cloud.
He has negroes work for him hate him,
wish him under the bullets of kennedydeath
OPEN FIRE FROM THE SCHOOL WINDOWS
these projectiles kill his mother plagued
by vulgar cancer, floating her dusty horoscope,
without the love even she thinks she needs, deadbitch,
Johnson's mother, walked all night holding hands
with a nigger, and stroked that nigger's
hard. Blew him downtown Newark 1928 . . . I got proof

Blank

This morning I feel like
sitting inside myself, like
a child like things do going nowhere
in the wind cooling it till the planet
explodes, this morning is like that the
aimless blowing which is everything, in the form
the million forms of emptiness which is everything
hot paradox
speeding into space
millions of miles   (the ant
"thinking") where can understanding
drop from where is settling under covers
listening to rain thought of flying out nothing
but the form of things, what we see to say responding
the ant the plant the lie the dog squatting in the universe

playing god
titling breath
loving things
these idle concepts of what the organism
feels, ow, feels, scream, feels, ahheeeeeeeee, feels, and that,
to be a
live,
is pitifully
insufficient

/Touch something and say love is a heart spitting blood
or skies eat fire shit suns say anything, touch me, say
something, name something, be something, not flying away
disappearing over fire horizons,

                all the heat of circumstance
                is cooled to physical science.
                touch-knowing, the explanation
                of why we were here, in the first
                motherfucking place, nobody asked,

xcept the form, our form, it
id, dropped, bled, shat, growed
 the sun under a pile of stinking
orlds,
          shit world, iron world, wood world, fire world (the world is
re), water world, all worlds lives fire flying speeds sounds, there
 no sound no thing no ideas no help hope or crying no thing no
hing, hear, no, with no sound, no voice or tongue beating lips
ays help love god walk cry time mope wills over crazy planes gysym
ays these things and they cannot crack the form, yes they do, crack
hat, form is something made up illusion, like anything, can't get
ast skin time, eye time, lip time, fuck time, where is time, and who
ies speeding in the sun, is why I'm here in time, my thought
o have never had a chance to be finite, or anything but live meat
nd image, live sound and image, thought, live shit, flying through the
niverse, there's no body
ere, all body, we try to figure this out, and fail, how cd it be
therwise.
          Believe in god, and get off the hot seat . . . otherwise
suffer motherfucker
in yr twisted up conceptual
pretensions, suffer, suffer, motherfucker
suffer these mathematical agonies, and never learn what you knew,
like whos here, anyway????

NEWSHIT

1.

The lovers speak to each other as if they were born
this second without anything but the world and their vision
which is a blue image of themselves, on 7th ave drinking, and
pretending to be the few things of value in the world.

We all need to tighten up. We all need each other. We all
need to stop lying and lock arms and look at each other
like black humans struggling with depraved eagles.

But the part of the whole that does not insist on its wholeness.
The dark, the shadow, the wealth of all our lives. Where is this
stored? And who is the master who corrupts the silence of our
beautiful consciousness.

2.

The heart
is love, is the soul, stretched out dying
they killed him he's dying stretched out cars
trampling his papers. An old dead man, wanted
life, killed in the street, screams, for light.

LIGHT LIGHT LIGHT LIGHT LIGHT LIGHT LIGHT LIGHT

he screams as if the world were a cellar, and nothing
in it reflected his needs.

> I am a mad nigger in love with everything
> You make it impossible to be myself in this
> place. Where can I go? Where is my self to
> live in this shaky universe.

> Oh love in the women of the world. Oh heart
> in the dungeon of the earth. Oh people who
> love me for being alive, help me, the world
> is changing, and I change, forever, with it.

Ghosts

In the dark town, out side the big city
in the dark town, the houses were pretty
in the dark town, whitey slept on television
all his women dead to the vision.

in the dark town, where three men waited
rain moon spun across the hot sky
in the dark town, the murderers rested
and looked at the things they hated.

When the sun in the dark town came up
three policemen staggered on their eyeballs
they lay dead in the cold new sun
they lay dead in the cold new sun

And when the wind blew
it was clean, and the walkers moved on
to another
scene

Song

I love you
love me
let's get together
& go to
sea
& stay
away
& fuck
all day
      please miss blackie
      can we split
      I'll kiss
      your mouth
      pull yr tit.
            Gently
            as sun
            as breeze
            where we go
            please
            miss
            blackie
            can we blow?

I Am Speaking of Future Good-ness and Social Philosophy

1.

When musicians say Cookin
it is food for the soul
that is being prepared, food
for the mad rain makers, black witches
good nature, whether rain everyday, or the
brightest of suns, every day, in our meat and
tubes, the newness and deadness of the central character.
Man is essential
to my philosophy,
man.

2.

The weather in spain could ride
in a train. Of generals and bishops
their assholes reamed with malice, the mountains
more beautiful than they,
though they be men. As the white man
is a man, no less his disqualification,
and subsequent reappearance as the beast
of the age. Men, no less. Though we must
finally kill them, rid the earth of them,
because they are a diseased species, but
recognized as God Fearing.

So we must become Gods.
Gigantic black ones.
And scare them back into the dirt.
With the heat of our words, and burning
stares. With the heat of our holy passion.

And then, with steel
with bricks
with garbage
dogs, purposes,
madness, tranquility,

weakness, strength, deadness
vitality, youth
and infirmity,
with knives and razors
and plans,

3.

(these aint clams
you eatin,
an ol' nigger
say, overhearing
this poem in my bowels,
ain't clams
dad.)

In short, everything that is magical, will respond, in men, if we
have the code
to their hearts.
Men are no more than
ourselves, other
places.
We should not despise our selves
but we must,
but never our brothers who are closer
to us than any
self,
ours
included.

We want to make things right.
We want to disappear except for our essence, which
is rightness.
We want to be nature and a natural thing.

Prepare for perfection.
All men who need it.

Prepare right positions.
All who deserve them.
Prepare for the real work of everybody.
Prepare for every real thing.
The mountains of dead will be sign of the times, invisible
suddenly, due to some beautiful tech
nology. Dead heaps of white ash, vanished, and the sun
allowed to shine. At the front door, baby, at the front
door, or any door, on anything, wail sun, beat on everybody good.

Lady Bug

The motherfuckin'
heart, of the
motherfuckin'
day, grows hot
as a bitch, on her
motherfuckin'
way, back home.

I want to go
back home.

I've got nothin'
against you. But I
got to get
back home.

THREE MOVEMENTS AND A CODA

THE QUALITY OF NIGHT THAT YOU HATE MOST IS ITS BLACK
AND ITS STARTEETH EYES, AND STICKS ITS STICKY FINGERS
IN YOUR EARS. RED NIGGER EYES LOOKING UP FROM A BLACK HOLE.
RED NIGGER LIPS TURNING KILLER GEOMETRY, LIKE HIS EYES ROLL UP
LIKE HE THOUGHT RELIGION WAS BEBOP.

                    LIKE HE THOUGHT RELIGION WAS
                    BEBOP . . . SIXTEEN KILLERS ON A
                    LIVE MAN'S CHEST . . . . THE LONE RANGER

IS DEAD.
THE SHADOW
IS DEAD.
ALL YOUR HEROES ARE DYING. J. EDGAR HOOVER WILL
SOON BE DEAD. YOUR MOTHER WILL DIE. LYNDON JOHNSON,

                    these are natural
                    things. No one is
                    threatening anybody
                    thats just the way life
                    is,
                        boss.

103

Red Spick talking to you from a foxhole very close to the
Vampire Nazis' lines. I can see a few Vampire Nazis moving very quickly
back and forth under the heavy smoke. I hear, and perhaps you do, in
the back ground, the steady deadly cough of mortars, and the light shatter
of machine guns.

BANZAI!!   BANZAI!!   BANZAI!!   BANZAI!!   BANZAI!!

Came running out of the drugstore window with
an electric alarm clock, and then dropped the motherfucker
and broke it. Go get somethin' else. Take everything in there.
Look in the cashregister. TAKE THE MONEY. TAKE THE MONEY. YEH.
TAKE IT ALL. YOU DONT HAVE TO CLOSE THE DRAWER. COME ON MAN, I SAW
A TAPE RECORDER BACK THERE.

These are the words of lovers.
Of dancers, of dynamite singers
These are songs if you have the
    music

T. T. Jackson sings

I fucked your mother
on top of a house
when I got through
she thought she was
Mickey Mouse.

I fucked your mother
under a tree
when it was over
she couldn't even pee

I fucked your mother
and she hollered OOOO
she thought I was
fu man chu

I fucked your mother
and she started to grin
then she found out
it wasn't even in.

In one battle

Three grey boys tracked us to an old house.
We saw them coming winding collecting the weather
in their slow movement. Grey also their day
which is their faces, and their understanding
of where we are.

Our murderous intentions
are what they hear, and think them thin whore hawks
brushing through the trees.

The other guys are already aiming
as greys snake towards the house.
I take a few seconds, to finish
these notes, now my fingers eagerly
toward the machine

Song Form

Morning uptown, quiet on the street,
no matter the distinctions that can be
made, quiet, very quiet, on the street.
Sun's not even up, just some kid and me,
skating, both of us, at the early sun, and
amazed there is grace for us, without our
having to smile too tough, or be very pleasant
even to each other. Merely to be mere, ly to be

Return of the Native

Harlem is vicious
modernism. BangClash.
Vicious the way its made.
Can you stand such beauty?
So violent and transforming.
The trees blink naked, being
so few. The women stare
and are in love with them
selves. The sky sits awake
over us. Screaming
at us. No rain.
Sun, hot cleaning sun
drives us under it.

The place, and place
meant of
black people. Their heavy Egypt.
(Weird word!) Their minds, mine,
the black hope mine. In Time.
We slide along in pain or too
happy. So much love
for us. All over, so much of
what we need. Can you sing
yourself, your life, your place
on the warm planet earth.
And look at the stones

the hearts, the gentle hum
of meaning. Each thing, life
we have, or love, is meant
for us in a world like this.
Where we may see ourselves
all the time. And suffer
in joy, that our lives
are so familiar.

EveryBody Out

What kind of voice   wd come to

this what kind of

need

wd

hurt
  so
much

thrown
   around
      &
         hurt

the shape was

this way

reveal a new

thing , a

new place for feeling, all

together

any
way

Sounding BELLOWING

Goodbye!

If we call
to ourselves
if we want to feel
who we are if
we want to love
what we can
be
come
into
a wide space
of heart
and hearts
meaning
we love (love love
(these are soft cries of feeling
can you help me, who are here w/ me can
you walk into my deep senses

I want you to understand the world
as I have come to understand it
I'll wait here a few seconds, please come

Black Bourgeoisie,

> has a gold tooth, sits long hours
> on a stool thinking about money.
> sees white skin in a secret room
> rummages his sense for sense
> dreams about Lincoln(s)
> conks his daughter's hair
> sends his coon to school
> works very hard
> grins politely in restaurants
> has a good word to say
> never says it
> does not hate ofays
> hates, instead, him self
> him black self

A Poem for Black Hearts

For Malcolm's eyes, when they broke
the face of some dumb white man, For
Malcolm's hands raised to bless us
all black and strong in his image
of ourselves, For Malcolm's words
fire darts, the victor's tireless
thrusts, words hung above the world
change as it may, he said it, and
for this he was killed, for saying,
and feeling, and being/ change, all
collected hot in his heart, For Malcolm's
heart, raising us above our filthy cities,
for his stride, and his beat, and his address
to the grey monsters of the world, For Malcolm's
pleas for your dignity, black men, for your life,
black man, for the filling of your minds
with righteousness, For all of him dead and
gone and vanished from us, and all of him which
clings to our speech black god of our time.
For all of him, and all of yourself, look up,
black man, quit stuttering and shuffling, look up,
black man, quit whining and stooping, for all of him,
For Great Malcolm a prince of the earth, let nothing in us rest
until we avenge ourselves for his death, stupid animals
that killed him, let us never breathe a pure breath if
we fail, and white men call us faggots till the end of
the earth.

Black Art

1965–1966

SOS

Calling black people
Calling all black people, man woman child
Wherever you are, calling you, urgent, come in
Black People, come in, wherever you are, urgent, calling
you, calling all black people
calling all black people, come in, black people, come
on in.

Black Art

Poems are bullshit unless they are
teeth or trees or lemons piled
on a step. Or black ladies dying
of men leaving nickel hearts
beating them down. Fuck poems
and they are useful, wd they shoot
come at you, love what you are,
breathe like wrestlers, or shudder
strangely after pissing. We want live
words of the hip world live flesh &
coursing blood. Hearts Brains
Souls splintering fire. We want poems
like fists beating niggers out of Jocks
or dagger poems in the slimy bellies
of the owner-jews. Black poems to
smear on girlemamma mulatto bitches
whose brains are red jelly stuck
between 'lizabeth taylor's toes. Stinking
Whores! We want "poems that kill."
Assassin poems, Poems that shoot
guns. Poems that wrestle cops into alleys
and take their weapons leaving them dead
with tongues pulled out and sent to Ireland. Knockoff
poems for dope selling wops or slick halfwhite
politicians Airplane poems, rrrrrrrrrrrrrrrr
rrrrrrrrrrrrrrr . . . tuhtuhtuhtuhtuhtuhtuhtuhtuh
. . . rrrrrrrrrrrrrrrr . . . Setting fire and death to
whities ass. Look at the Liberal
Spokesman for the jews clutch his throat
& puke himself into eternity . . . rrrrrrrr
There's a negroleader pinned to
a bar stool in Sardi's eyeballs melting
in hot flame Another negroleader
on the steps of the white house one
kneeling between the sheriff's thighs
negotiating cooly for his people.

Agggh . . . stumbles across the room . . .
Put it on him, poem. Strip him naked
to the world! Another bad poem cracking
steel knuckles in a jewlady's mouth
Poem scream poison gas on beasts in green berets
Clean out the world for virtue and love,
Let there be no love poems written
until love can exist freely and
cleanly. Let Black People understand
that they are the lovers and the sons
of lovers and warriors and sons
of warriors Are poems & poets &
all the loveliness here in the world

We want a black poem. And a
Black World.
Let the world be a Black Poem
And Let All Black People Speak This Poem
Silently
or LOUD

Incident

He came back and shot. He shot him. When he came
back, he shot, and he fell, stumbling, past the
shadow wood, down, shot, dying, dead, to full halt.

At the bottom, bleeding, shot dead. He died then, there
after the fall, and the speeding bullet, tore his face
and blood sprayed fine over the killer and the grey light.

Pictures of the dead man, are everywhere. And his spirit
sucks up the light. But he died in darkness darker than
his soul and everything tumbled blindly with him dying

down the stairs.

We have no word

on the killer, except he came back, from somewhere
to do what he did. And shot only once into his victim's
stare, and left him quickly when the blood ran out. We know

the killer was skillful, quick, and silent, and that the victim
probably knew him. Other than that, aside from the caked sourness
of the dead man's expression, and the cool surprise in the fixture

of his hands and fingers, we know nothing.

For a lady i know.

Talk the talk I need
you, as you resurrect
your consciousness above
the streets, as you walk
with me, and lay
with me, and wonder
what is on
my mind. Oh talk, talk,
lady, and remind yrself
that you are dealing
with a spirit, deal, madam,
in your bigassed smiling eyes
in the world of real things—
as I have pronounced the life
in our fingers, real, so you must be
and grow to love me, as I must, of
course, finally, fall on my knees,
with love for you.

Poem for HalfWhite College Students

Who are you, listening to me, who are you
listening to yourself? Are you white or
black, or does that have anything to do
with it? Can you pop your fingers to no
music, except those wild monkies go on
in your head, can you jerk, to no melody,
except finger poppers get it together
when you turn from starchecking to checking
yourself. How do you sound, your words, are they
yours? The ghost you see in the mirror, is it really
you, can you swear you are not an imitation greyboy,
can you look right next to you in that chair, and swear,
that the sister you have your hand on is not really
so full of Elizabeth Taylor, Richard Burton is
coming out of her ears. You may even have to be Richard
with a white shirt and face, and four million negroes
think you cute, you may have to be Elizabeth Taylor, old lady,
if you want to sit up in your crazy spot dreaming about dresses,
and the sway of certain porters' hips. Check yourself, learn who it is
speaking, when you make some ultrasophisticated point, check yourself,
when you find yourself gesturing like Steve McQueen, check it out, ask
in your black heart who it is you are, and is that image black or white,

you might be surprised right out the window, whistling dixie on the way in

A School of Prayer

A hollow eye sees moons dance
music in the pupil as it studies the changing
   world, We are all beautiful (except white
people, they are full of, and made of
   shit) O black people full of illusions
and weird power. O my loves and my heart
   pumping black blood screaming through
my thickened veins.

                    Do not obey their laws
                    which are against God
                    believe brother, do not
                    ever think any of that
                    cold shit they say is
                    true. They are against
                    the law. Their "laws"
                    are filthy evil, against
                    almighty God. They are
                    sick to be against God,
                    against the animals and sun,
                    against thought and feeling
                    against the world as it most commonly
                    is. That is they are against
                    beauty. Do not let them show you
                    a beer can, except believe their profundity
                    is as easily read. Do not believe or shelter them.
                    Do not let them eat your children. Do not believe
                    or shelter them, or shelter their slickbullshit
                    for one second in your heart.

The eye sees. The I. The self. Which passes out and into
the wind. We are so beautiful we talk at the same time
and our breathing is harnessed to divinity.

Movie

Of the fire, or the red bursts, eyes hearts
yellow girls explosive disillusions. Oh yes
the fire, the running, and pistols cracking.
Of the fire, the smoke, the yells, and disaster. The
dead babies, and blown resolutions, sweeps prat prat wood
snapping, things giving way. Where to go. What . . . what
the fuck, to do?

     Lead out. To the side. Green field passing.
Under, and shadows, streaking there wild wild and good (the day
too.

This is a sudden abandon. My heart with me. All presses.

The story of goodface, the elf. Who had no mother or father, but
stumbled through the mud of common disaster. A lily in his ear.
Great god, hear the tumbled niggers scream. And disaster. disaster.
The low blow of your own sensitivity. The scum burial, and shadows.

We were without. And it came. The cold blue. And
casual stances. The white people's grace. Their finely etched
lives. Where were our own? Who
were we? Why did we lead lives concealed in nigger code? What
penalty, that we knew so deeply as the sea its waves and wetness
the penalty, the dead look at the world, our consciousness so
accused us. But the word words crash picturebelched blind the
sun. I am a son, and father. The bright thing, the necessary,
even in this ugly white world.

     How did we get out?
     What did we do?
     (People growl. Growl. I'm
      growling. Growl. Biting this
      lady on the neck. Growl. Feel
      so much got to

get it in, feel so much, and mean so much, mean, and
feel myself, straining, then blast out smash fingertip bomb
dart poison sailing african landscape death of the final
missionary.

    Help. He is screaming, and I am beating the life
out of him. Help, he is sore . . . beat . . . beat, his
grey pulpy shit from his head "stickies the floor"
pastorals above the clouds anyway, exploded lovers

Biography

Hangs.
whipped
blood
striped
meat pulled
clothes ripped
slobber
feet dangled
pointing
noised
noise
churns
face
black sky
and moon
leather night
red
bleeds
drips
ground
sucks
blood
hangs
life wetting
sticky
mud

laughs
bonnets
wolfmoon
crazyteeth

hangs

hangs

granddaddy
granddaddy, they tore

his
neck

The Racist

The heart I hold
is mine, and I am
everybody's. All the humans. I
let them have my heart.

(the old positions

like addresses, lose us,
mail piles up
check made out to marion brown t/o where
is love, after

All.

We want everything. We want
to feel
everything. Vashti, we want to love
all that demands love
to survive.

(new things
like black
like feeling
like inside kingly wealth

like
the world
or love
or all that the shadowy beings
are deprived of. All the hair turning under their
necks. Pimples, which they pick open
with
safety
pins. Am I and Am I.

Do not be a thing, with
out
yr
sense
delay
for
    ever, thing, no feel
    ing, or, the burst of morning
    yellow fields of day day sun, oh good sweet time

    I lean away from here, from what you see
into, out
of, a far churning burning
of atoms, away, pure vector space without a move
complete, and there, and here, and touch me
OOOOOOOOOOOOOO
the swing's complete
the hand, through air, my hair
's a cloud, just moisture cools the passage
a line of dry spells from here to start again

The sign

Leans
we are worlds of leaning, talling, reaching, with
reaching with, what we reach for already
in back, of us, reaching
for and through
the space
we take

spake adventure pacts boys and dogs, dirty niggers, fly
speak sound sunny walking dogs grassiron, initials, signs
street crack sound round universe green stains paint . . . round rounded
ded lamp shape of bird winged gone sound moan love god job
is abbreviated no cars dead paper and metal, stone and windows, sun
and the fellahs sings so ething flying leaves banged in the bowl,
hinges then calypso lost cities of bass there we golden bough leaning
with the torn danny bow hidden stick of africa behind the dollarsigns and
skulls to twist the little halfwhite colored girls giggling at everything
and everything is a sad and not a funny the dangling metal buddha monk, the
priests behind, gold ticket of nigger beethoven railing mad commerce to
wave red bright leans a brick and boy together lace and bamboo cut and
shorn between the voice and steps of talk hurting each other tiny voices
drone bad parts of the chord, names, whistles, breath, concentrate the yoga
strength and beauty lazy june whistles bye bye a prayer song sweet moan

Evil Nigger Waits for Lightnin'

Alone, at night, with all the world
not watching, around me,
who for the understanding
intended, the love
withheld,
would be lost in the blackness
of self-nights
howling like something
or scurrying behind iceboxes
like something
would be them things
in my conscious
ness, or waddlegirls
full of invisible demands
they are children the world will tell you
only children, lost dreams, that you should love
if you can, from the tower of Headlust, you they moan
should always adore them, lost feeling, should love and
take yrself through any change to understand their blankness.

Alone at night the world disappears breathing over my head weeping it
is lost or unappreciated. It says I do not love it. And sends its dopey
messengers to touch me right. The world, the world says, is full of love
can you find it, can you enter, and remain, grow strong with it beautiful
thing
in the rain, the world,
these sent things whisper
mice, fucked ladies, whisps of cloud
still visible four oclock in the nighttime
for the expanding or retracting dying or just coming
thing
we will always
be.

The Astronomers,
The Philosophers,
The Crowd, of them,

Things, These dangerous feelers, for understanding,
now that I am alone so much I can manage to
hear another thing
singing through my face
describing the arc
and the constant
return . . .
> way out now,
> describing its own voice
> its
> reason

The woman thing

We call love sometimes blank
and longed for. We call love, or
anything, comes up, sweeps by,
causes the movement by which we
feel
  sometimes it's like flesh only
  and we come and come and come
  or the feeling built between two
  hearts, can it be perfect, can it last,

can you find someone in this nation willing to live with
pure impression, and the world of essences, sometimes focusing
to permit a man, to be seen, sliding through the world

and this is a personal plea.

Red light

The only thing we know is the thing
we turn out to be, I don't care what
you think, its true, now you think
your way out of this

American Ecstasy

"Loss of Life or Both Feet or Both Hands or Both Eyes .... The Principal Sum

Loss of One Hand and One Foot .... The Principal Sum

Loss of One Hand and One Eye or One Foot and One Eye .... The Principal Sum

Loss of One Hand or One Foot .... One half The Principal Sum

Loss of One Eye .... One fourth The Principal Sum"

Little Brown Jug

Who are you?
A lost brother.
A singer. A song
I lost, almost, sat up
one night, itched
till it came
to me, cried
one night, happy
that it played
through me.

Little Brown Jug. Nigger Brother.
Dust singer in
the shadow of old
fences. Companion, of melody
rhythm
turned around heart runs
climbed & jumped screaming
WE ARE GODS, as we
sailed years through the firmament
landing beside a
garage, Dear brother, song
slides the streets, circles the cold,
sweats on summer fruit, Oh I
love my black energy &
lost brother father serenade
me, as world-solo, the spirits
bubble, loft, & say
where you are. I suffer
to hear you so tough
& know all the spooks
who need to.

Attention Attention

Attention Attention

(at tension, we niggers work
supremesmiraclesimpressions, &c.

we work our shit for spite all night
"He sd to the grocer, quite unaware that
he had been overheard, 'Go fly a kike,' " being
in Harlem, an old dutch settlement full of
brown hardbacked bugs, and drooling irishmens.)

Attention Attention
Attention Attention

All greys must be terminated immediately
Project cutoff date moved up Fifty Years

End of species must be assured. (Repeat)
End of species must be assured.

All greys must be terminated immediately
End of species must be assured.

Part of The Doctrine

Body, rupa, Body, rupa, Body, rupa, Body, rupa,
Matter a body flies. Mantra a matter, a rupa the
other, a body, no, matter, derv bells hums forever
twee night, the jings gles, the raiches street gag, body
walks the milky way, smiles again, the fat jolliness of the man,
the prophet, the inextricable, limit, loss, set, the balance, of
the man, who has reached beyond the matter, earth, beyond the merely
infinite, cosmic conceit the barreling heavens, in his hand were they
funny laughing east barrels, slithinsinuate his dirty white halls. Would
that heaven heaven calls-ing would that comma karma between divide the
coolness of the tone to tell what is the reason for goodness and evil, would
that thee, wood dat the other see, cut dat barge steal that mail cut that jar
l stem, cut that broke beat and beat broke beak

is the body speaksing, speaks, from meat of more or all
there is, from the body, rupa, the body, of more or all
the smooth line up of opposites, as were the landscape blooms
in the high heat, at the high speed, at the pulse light, all terms
decisions made, Huge Beast of the Night, awake to be the whole
of creation, the thing breathing, a breast silhouette, under supercool
new moons of turning into

W. W.

Back home the black women are all beautiful,
and the white ones fall back, cutoff from 1000
years stacked booty, and Charles of the Ritz
where jooshladies turn into billy burke in blueglass
kicks. With wings, and jingly bew-teeful things.
The black women in Newark are fine. Even with all that grease
in their heads. I mean even the ones where the wigs
slide around, and they coming at you 75degrees off course.
I could talk to them. Bring them around. To something.
Some kind of quick course, on the sidewalk, like Hey baby
why don't you take that thing off yo' haid. You look like
Miss Muffett in a runaway ugly machine. I mean. Like that.

Camptown Ladies Sing Dis Song

Lorenzo Jones
and his wife bell. Lived
in hell. In the jingles six oclock
a hip enough time. We eating blue peas
on the register. Heat coming up our
gowns. Why did Lorenzo Jones
talk like that. From walking, jerking
off, or letting people
walk away from him. A nice brown
house this dude lived
in. With knobs, and green
stripes. I loved
the music too.

Very Fine

Can you carry
down the street, in the sun
as a girl with
her child
for the first
as the blast of planes
and their logic
collec
tors, and theirs
dogs, and their
souls, mystics, rising above
their carry down the street
as a girl with
a child
so beautiful
walks slewfoot
with shorts
shiny hair
is the world then
all or nothing,
              where you are
              or where you fall
         will you touch i want yes touch touch
      the thing you need, this is not only for me
              who enters
              the movies
              must sit
              in the dark

CIVIL RIGHTS POEM

Roywilkins is an eternal faggot
His spirit is a faggot
his projection
and image, this is
to say, that if i ever see roywilkins
on the sidewalks
imonna
stick half my sandal
up his
ass

Labor and Management

This is the nature of change
that it must seem jagged and
convulsed, but remain the smooth speed
of universal wisdom.

2;
    We will not weep for any weakness
    we will be stronger another way
    which is the real one centuries ago
    to see it develop, like comfort
    on this coolish
    planet.

We will not adjust we will be
just, to the adjust of speed
turns and the like. We will be
like earth and stay where we are
fertile for flowers and shit
or lovers and shit
or bright new black children
of the world.

We love to be here, which is why
we don't die.

the deadly eyes
are stars!

fools
say, i've sd it

and come to regret the white filth
jamming thru my veins, come to hate

the quiet well disposed "beauties" of the
word, without substance, even opposed
to it, as black hearts pumping through eyes

cannot see stars, cannot see skies, cannot see
anything, except the truth, the fat bulging lunatic

eyes, of the white man, which are not stars, and his
face, not sky, and him self, no God, just another lame

in love with him self, at everybody elses expense. Why dont

somebody kill the motherfucker? Why dont somebody jam his head
in his own shit? Why are all you chumps standing around

doing nothing? Letting this creap tapdance on your dreams.

These Cats Rolling on a Cardboard Box

      Where's there the
missing
of it, the wheres
hold of rolling
the streets
hold of smell in the
hold of taste touch
in the beyond what they be this five sense
we has or
spose
to
i cant say i'm alone
with 4thousan
colored folks on this street
alone
defying chafaggy's
sin-suds
and they's
in the, hold of
the, taste and they fly guitar laughs

of the bigbutt lady
holding and being there being there
all
of us, loving each other we play
these sincerities, evening now, we show
off, cut
the fool
early evening early
sun-ra too, a nigger, we love
for all the corny shit we see
or have put
on us,

      can you understand

      these

      dribble

          dee

             bibble

                dees

                  these warm street shoobies
                  my soul gets off behind

NEWARK LATER

In the black crime hearts. Where they beat firecracker blue sidewindow nights the ladies wait for you in bars, and people laugh, the people try to sleep, or stay up all night locked up in something. These nights each night, another face, or stray bullet. Or what is the actual sound in your heart when you touch somebody, and sparks burn up your loveseat. If we were walking up Market Street. Phantoms. Lock clock help, kiss me! There was a junkie, old thing. And the alleys, and people to talk to, to pity, to lie about. And sit somewhere in the dark kissing somebody's cross. Somebody's lay. Dee shit is that bad. And wide, and good (where are you?? call us?? You alright?? Who, I wanted that question answered too, before, the jell, and crying, the not yet complete redisintegration, and return, billions dying blowing in each second, like an old blueeyed man, convinced forever he is a devil. Help Me. Please. I'm spirit man my fingers warm me. Heart roaming african round eyed trek bamboom i'm tired through the jungle, the mountains, where they hung yr lord, I went up checking, for a while, up up and away.

Ka 'Ba

A closed window looks down
on a dirty courtyard, and black people
call across or scream across or walk across
defying physics in the stream of their will

Our world is full of sound
Our world is more lovely than anyone's
tho we suffer, and kill each other
and sometimes fail to walk the air

We are beautiful people
with african imaginations
full of masks and dances and swelling chants
with african eyes, and noses, and arms,
though we sprawl in grey chains in a place
full of winters, when what we want is sun.

We have been captured,
brothers. And we labor
to make our getaway, into
the ancient image, into a new

correspondence with ourselves
and our black family. We need magic
now we need the spells, to raise up
return, destroy, and create. What will be

the sacred words?

The Spell

The Spell The SPELL THE S P E L L L L L L L L L L L !
Away and sailing in warm space. The eyes of God-our on us
in us. The Spell. We are wisdom, reaching for itself. We are
totals, watch us, watch through yourself, and become the whole
universe at once so beautiful you will become, without having
moved, or gone through a "change," Except to be moving with the world,
at that incredible speed, with all the genius of a tree.

Beautiful Black Women . . .

Beautiful black women, fail, they act. Stop them, raining.
They are so beautiful, we want them with us. Stop them, raining.
Beautiful, stop raining, they fail. We fail them and their lips
stick out perpetually, at our weakness. Raining. Stop them. Black
queens, Ruby Dee weeps at the window, raining, being lost in her
life, being what we all will be, sentimental bitter frustrated
deprived of her fullest light. Beautiful black women, it is
still raining in this terrible land. We need you. We flex our
muscles, turn to stare at our tormentor, we need you. Raining.
We need you, reigning, black queen. This/ terrible black ladies
wander, Ruby Dee weeps, the window, raining, she calls, and her voice
is left to hurt us slowly. It hangs against the same wet glass, her
sadness and age, and the trip, and the lost heat, and the grey cold
buildings of our entrapment. Ladies. Women. We need you. We are still
trapped and weak, but we build and grow heavy with our knowledge. Women.
Come to us. Help us get back what was always ours. Help us. women. Where
are you, women, where, and who, and where, and who, and will you help
us, will you open your bodysouls, will you lift me up mother, will you
let me help you, daughter, wife/lover, will you

148

The penalty is death, for death
to walk up cold paths with fake light
splintering water, patchy thighs rubbed together
under the spoils of (they think) the universe. All
except spirit, up the concrete under glass, they come in
and look at other beings like them, parading, sleeping, deathly
colorless tin cans, ashes in peach juice, lipstick cigars jammed
in their eggs. Brecht speaks and they cannot hear. Their own species
accuses, and the blue veins bulge in their ankles, the jewelry cold cancer
identifying these diseased creatures, slobbering over humanity.

A portrait of them while they rule the world. For my Brothers dead living and
yet unborn. This year 1966, in their measure, almost two thousand years since
they hung this ol' jew, and made Sidney Poitier carry his cross. (The landscape
from that hill was marvelous, you could get papaya juice and knishes, nudist movies
and cheap flashy clothes.) In this year, when they are still dealing death. Some sleep
holding their breath in the urine air. Some march on roofs shitting on everything. Some
hold hands with beautiful niggers, rubbing their rings into the niggers chests, the
jews send their girls, a hundred of their best, each year into the black world, to
perform the ritual. The glazed eyes of the victim, hears the drums, war drums, and
thinks about museums, or interesting queers, or eating pussy. The drums go on, the wind
batters his head, these hundred sailing vampires settle their ears to the black man's balls
their radio tongues to his thigh. The penalty is death, for death. You walk with them
hypnotized niggers. You crawl up in the dark stomach of a monster, and the blood feels good
running in your mouth. You smile. You sit and say intelligence to animals. You hold hands
with dumb material, and lose all light

Lerve

HAB YOU EBER BEEN BLACK AND SWEATED COME
IN THE DARK BITCH CLUTCHON YOU LIFE WHISPER
SEE HER NOW THE DARK BROWN BLACK LOVE DIDNYU
SEE HER BLACK HANGING CLOTHES IN THE JUNE
DIDN YOU EBER WAKE UP SHITTIFIED AND STRETCHIFIED
AND LAWD LAWD ALL EARTH WORLD DEIFIED, NIGHT DID IT
AND I'M HUMPIN LIKE LORD MOVE MENT HIS SELF, FOR
THE DAY TIME, AND ME THE NIGHT BEING MOVING HIS CREATIONS,
AND SHE HANGING UP CLOTHES LONG AND BLACK AND THE WIND
REMEMBERING ALL THE SHIT WE SCREAMED AT IT LAST EVENIN

150

Trespass Into Spirit

aaaaaaaaaaaaaaaaaaaahahaaha ahahaaneene neeeeneeaahaaahneeeahhh

wooooouhhhahhhhheeehhhhhhhhh ohhhhh ahahahahahahahauahuahuah

uuuuaaahhhhhh   uuuuuwwwassssaaaaaaaaaaaaaaaaa

dehhhhh dehhhh dadadadadad ehhhhhehehehehehe

dedededededededededededededed   aaaaaaaaaaaaa

—A Chant to rise with all

with all rising thru and let the scope

diry jsolekks eoɔ fjoel fjkks ei   OO dkkle;pspekl''melks;;a;;sll

a;; ,ome. tje rpse. asmd;;e; rwodespimd;;s kek$\frac{1}{2}$w $\frac{1}{2}\frac{1}{2}$

k;;;;a ;;;dkp

the machines head is gone

red noise dirty fanning hurts love test run love and

they will not save serve spake to rise with over they test love in stone

and love to be there shirts fail me, naked will hurt rise the shine and round

of wake wake moisture and sun, describe me, angels!!

For Tom Postell, Dead Black Poet

1.

You told me, you told me
a thousand years ago. And the white man thing
you screamed on me, all true, and the walk
across from dead Trujillo, who grinned at us
into yr dead room. Only the winebottles lived
and sparkled and sailed easily for completion. You
screamed and slobbered on me, to hear you. And I
didn't. Shacked up with a fat jew girl. Talking about
Shakespeare, I didn't hear
you brother. Pussy Eater, you said, and another nigger
said the same, and the blood flowed down my face, and Lear
laughed at his new fool. I wallowed in your intestines,
brother, stole, and changed, your poems. And rode was rode
by the cows and intelligent snakes of the age. While they
killed you, while they ran you down third avenue, "talking
through your mouth," I didn't understand. You had your hand
clapped tightly on your lips. Your eyes rolling rolled up
Sanpaku dying. "The jews are talking
through my mouth." And I was horrified so niggerish and
unheroic was your death. And jews talked through my mouth,
and I used your wine fume soul. I laughed among the beasts
and meateaters. I strode with them, played with them, thought myself
one with them, and jews were talking through
my mouth. I had not the sense to stop them.
A thousand years ago you told me. Horrified beyond breathing. Stiff
with terror at the kikish evil pulling at your lips. I should have screamed
for you, brother. I should have climbed to the tops of the buildings and
screamed and dropped niggerbombs on their heads. For my dead. For my
dead brother. Who told me. A thousand years ago.

2.

Now I know what the desert thing was. Why they fled from us
into their caves. Why they hate me now. Why Martin Duberman (what
kind of man . . .) A *Duber* man, dobiedoo . . .   Why they hate me,

having seen them as things, and the resistance to light, and the
heart of goodness sucked off, vampires, flying in our midst, at the
corner, selling us our few horrible minutes of discomfort and frus
tration. Smile, jew. Dance, jew. Tell me you love me, jew. I got
something for you now though. I got something foryou, like you dig,
I got. I got this thing, goes pulsating through black everything
universal meaning. I got the extermination blues, jewboys. I got
the hitler syndrome figured. What that simpleton meant. He can't
stand their desert smell, their closeness to the truth. What
Father Moses gave them, and lifted them off their hands. A Magic
Charm. A black toe sewn in their throats. To talk, to get up
off their hands, and walk, like men (they will tell you.
So come for the rent, jewboys, or come ask me for a book, or
sit in the courts handing down yr judgments, still I got something
for you, gonna give it to my brothers, so they'll know what your *whole*
story is, then one day, jewboys, we all, even my wig wearing mother
gonna put it on you all at once,

Form Is Emptiness

e word Raaaaaaaaaaaaaaaaaaaaaaaaaaaaaaaaaaaaaaaaaaaaaaaaaaaaa

all its per

utations:

      Raaaaa

           aaaaaaaaaaaaaaahhhhhhhhhhhhhhhhhhh

           Allaaaaaaaaaahhhhhhhhh

           Dam

           Ballaaaaahhhhhhhhhhhhhh

              Chakra, the Buddha, returned

              Sankaracharya, Ahhllahhhhh

                  Dam

              Baaahhhhlaaahhh

                      is not word

                      is no lines

                      no meanings

Raaaaaaaaaahhhhhhhhhh the unchanging,

Caucasian Devachan

In the dark the elf who had inherited the material world sat in a dark room with only himself, with only his eyes and his stomach and tried to look out the windows but there were no windows, and no light, no sound, just the things he sat there surrounded by the things of the world, transformed by their deadness, transfixed, yet leaning to listen as if there were still sounds he could hear or objects he could see, he would lay down in his subjective stillness, new worlds humming out of range of his outmoded ears.

Like a bag of powder death stillness sit at a level of wood half in half out of shadow, like the world itself, the elf was no longer anything but the actual elf, his body's energy and deathray stilled, in the final turn into darkness. Where the retribution, that he walks with now, the brokenness of the dwarf, the maimed horrible elf in the streets with cold downcast despair hoarded in this future wet cellar like a shriveled bear sleep in a log, the little thing sits

The Rainy Night I Went Away

This is heavy elecgric thunder
speaking on the hero's chest
in gold, glaring shit, the juke
bucks little wholes in the sess
stem, little craves and a spastic
momma give the earth and sky, the
whole shit of splitting. to pay
the price, for a lil innocent
adventure. You cant think thats
Fuji? her stomach? no I'm no travler
en terre, my ass is broke with what I
want to know, being a jabbing steel
critic of darkness, the gold brightness
flying flowing so fast shit so muther
fucking fast, fast fast whew, gone
shit
Critic of the splitting shit
and the dog
the down
and the real stockings on milkmomma
cookie prize winners
who are spenders, like the rest
of us the time
this takes
this round
in where hurting is trouble specific

clean out my pockets then
clean out my ass
my brain
trample and turn and burn your corny shit
but i will be cool
even after i
die
and none of your shit
will even be remembered except in the portals of all faith

and placement of the animal vegetable mineral thing. i mean
where folks is. what they think and build because
they feel that corny
shit is right. i wanted to be successful
like the rest
of the objects.
So here's a tip
romantics, be on time in your adventure
be on top of the tables with a bottle in your hand
if you want to survive that way,
otherwise retire to your invisible conning tower
thats the house they have the telescope going in
lay then
like they say lay, my man
and wait cold stony eyed
for evolution.

Babylon Revisited

The gaunt thing
with no organs
creeps along the streets
of Europe, she will
commute, in her feathered bat stomach-gown
with no organs
with sores on her insides
even her head
a vast puschamber
of pus(sy) memories
with no organs
nothing to make babies
she will be the great witch of euro-american legend
who sucked the life
from some unknown nigger
whose name will be known
but whose substance will not ever
not even by him
who is dead in a pile of dopeskin

This bitch killed a friend of mine named Bob Thompson
a black painter, a giant, once, she reduced
to a pitiful imitation faggot
full of American holes and a monkey on his back
slapped airplanes
from the empire state building

May this bitch and her sisters, all of them,
receive my words
in all their orifices like lye mixed with
cocola and alaga syrup

feel this shit, bitches, feel it, now laugh your
hysterectic laughs
while your flesh burns
and your eyes peel to red mud

Message From The NAACP

I wanted something, you know, in
what you thought sitting suns galunkah
deeray shun of plove, oh I'm comin' to see

what I can do for yall, and who'm I, ol Roy
Wilkins, another that bunch, you see me, look at
my suit, yah, you digit? the suit, my man, this come
from Brook Brother, and cost, flesh and the dead blowed out belly
of a puertorican chinaman. I'm cool, jidrool, I'm on the top floor
in the office, with all the voices below on those fucking marquees
I'm roy oh hi, oh hellow, oh hi, oh will you excuse me, oh, and
pull down the drawers gently at night with a moon and a pecabooly
boo. I'm human like everybody else. I mean all you white people. All
you *stars*, and co-stars, and supporting actors, cause where I come from
the only shit's the steady ugly drone of leaking lives. Shit yous 'pect
me to dig despair?????

That Mighty Flight

My brother, Bigger Thomas, son of

Poor Richard, father, of poor

lost jimmy, locked together all

of us, wringing our hands in the dark.

Lost to our selves and our people, that we find,

just few moments of life and light let it come

down, lord, that we love life more than all life

and want it, want our selves, and our black soul nation

to love us as great strong prophets and heroes, but weak

lord, we weak as flesh, fall sometimes, Bigger laughed

when the old jew left him, "a wry bitter smile," dug

we were flying, and his father, and brother, and the son's

son, all rising, lord, to become the thing you told us

Madness

The white man

at best

is

corny

but who is to say it how is the
who how is the black man? to say
what when he sits biting his ass
in the sun, or laid cross a puddle
for snailtitty to cross over, how
and with what logic and moral who
is fed by the meanest of streams
will we move, or will we be merely
proud, as the best, yet with will
to be ego, or self same mean bastards
corrupting our inch of despair. To try,
what, for what, who will appreciate, who
will benefit, to desert is no different or better,
they all have deserted and sit in the sun under a sign
spirits waving through summer and fall spirits in the cold
place of our crucifixion, break the man-head off the sign
it is a cross, a double dirty cross, to hang your civilization

what can we say, open your mouth
do your lips, read, look
why I want to confront you
why you are a child or dead old man
how can i move when they will not move with me
is this the dark room
is this the closed door
the empty face
the vanished strength

just big mouf niggers alright just big floats
alligator heads in the mardi gras, dance and cry
shadows of living deadmen, dance and cry

sit up scream in church, under the blinking sign
of the times, a bar, a pignostril parlor

proud of what
of what what tell me yeh tell me motherfucker
what are you proud, any of you, tell me, what
for being slaves, for dying, for watching them feeling them
chop you up vomit you out lie to you kill burn tear your eyes
out and your ears, with your soul string dangled under the
same cold sun, your soul string, which suffered and you left
and dont care, to be cool with tony bennett, an old nigger man
for you now, and the cars, for you now, or the slow pause of death,
for you junky whore red head fag twist bump jam caress the image
of stupidness, fried haid skinny bitch laughing at god, and "i'd
don't know," har har har, with pigs to give her chilrun, and
nothing but heartache since they ain't too proud to beg

for what even you long bushhead with the little glasses
a style of yr own to carry the futility more righteously
but no matter, the same criss cross ugly jealousy and white
vomit sometimes for brains. we poets drummers hornplayers, nationalists
running our corny shit on a people standin in the sun
rotting rotting for centuries destined to die with the
white man destined to die with the white man destined
to die with the white man, the white man we say we hate
the white man we want to kill the whiteman who kills us
the white man, WHO AT BEST IS VERY VERY CORNY DUDE
to we die you will at the best to very die destined falling
ground-face hands burned in the windows fall corny die
the legend will be
the suffering and sacrifice will be
gone
lost
done
never
no one will remember
except the lost servants died with their masters

when the rest of the spiritual world got fullup
with corniness and death
the eternal life
we know we are
lostdie
heart fall
up, "i'm hurt, help me, no stay with me nigger,
die with me nigger
look jump off the building
with me, nigger, jump jump
look how we fall through space, nigger,
sign you up to play at newport
you can run the jazzmobile
you want to go to lincoln center
look i'll give you the goddam academy award
letme slap your face dianne, let me, die with you, off the
building, falling, hurt, gone
lost
done
never
no one will remember
Hi Yo Silver . . . Away!!" we die with the white man
the buildings stick us in the heart
we die
with
oh no
please
not
not that
not with
oh please
can we
oh
not
lost
yest-

a ha,
a ha, ha, ha
a ha, ha, ha, ha, ha, ha, ha, hahahahahahahahahahahahaha

kyrie kyrie kyrie elision

Ballad of the Morning Streets

The magic of the day is the morning
I want to say the day is morning high
and sweet, good
morning.

The ballad of the morning streets, sweet
voices turns
of cool warm weather
high around the early windows grey to blue
and down again amongst the kids and
broken signs, is pure love magic, sweet day
come into me, let me live with you
and dig your blazing

They have outposts

(a poem for some turnedaround niggers)

Passion. Use it.
Use black passion.
Strong bump necks.
He paints, and lives in Portland Oregon use him
white man. Use his skin and rolling eyes. His reaching
hands. Pump the poison, in, white man. Vibrate Virginia Mayo's fools' gold pussy
cold wind makes the fire dance winter shadows thousands of years developing television
in the caves, use his reds and yellows use his long stride, look through the snow, white
man, hold out in your venereal humor through the million year winter, food shadow flits
across the dead earth. A black writer rabbit. Too close to the Italians. Huddled from
the weather with an albino praying mantis. Even this insect has a pussy, a white anti-
room, where my friend, in his yellow flesh defines the insect world. How can I reach
him. Must I call his name. Must I call all your names lost brothers?

                                                              Leave the beast
in its snowy den. Sneak out in the night and run till youre warm. Till your body sweats
and the world makes sense again. Run out from in there, brother. Save yourself.

167

I said it

There are facts lodged in our world.
Incident. That Japan is Japan, not Nippon
(Or Nihon) because some stupid italian
could not understand what the word was, and so
brought this ignorance of the world back to his
dirty home. The word, or,
              The style,
              or, "jus cannot rember those foreign tongues"
the white man's isolation, like the sun slicking thousands
of miles of snow into ice where such philosophies were dreamed
up. In those barren caves, on those inhuman cold scenes the white
man's hairy ancestors made their first baby gesture to fuck up
the world. The cold could not sustain human life, witness the
dogjawed cracker of the west. Who is so cold would wipe his behind
on the souls of men.

Bludoo Baby, Want Money, and Alligator Got It to Give

say day lay day may fay come some bum'll
take break jake make fake lay day some bum'll
say day came break snow mo whores red said they'd
lay day in my in fay bed to make bread for jake
limpin in the hall with quiverin stick
he's hiney raised, in a car by the curb,
licking his yellow lips, yellow snow yellow bubs
yellow eyes lookin at the dark, hears his whisper
says, "come down goily i give you a stick . . . da da da
  come down goily i give you a pinch . . . da da da
  come down goily i sit in my car . . . da da da
  come down goily to where we grey guys are . . . da da da . . .
           da da da . . .
           da da da . . .
           da da da . . ."

she's not thinkna him, seein him, seen people like him
dazed out there, suckin heavy vapors, her but throw off,
like stick-it-in nitetime, for the dough, chile, for the money
baby, look at him down there, lookn up at me . . . da da da
she and jake
look

da cuppd flame
fat claws, motor batting
outside miss workamo's house.

shd she go down she's pulling the coat
gainst the wind, will she let him, ol good guy
get in.
for the dough
mr tom
for your woman
in the mirror

shakin like a storm

psst oh miss, oh miss, oh oh, yellow, vapor butt got him
hung out the window
look down
jake jr.
and mr roy
there, look kin you help . . . da da da
kin you give me
somethin
can you make me
beautiful
with your bullshit
can you
love me
nigger
she askin us, jake jr
sis betty, where we at, at the pin of the stare, curld flag of misery,

oh the hip walk on that chile
fat sister, swashing that heavy ass
psst psst
oh miss miss,

yellow
cloud it up
stick it in
and jab down
under the wheel . . . da da da

miss
oh miss

stumbling down the stairs
when she turns to go back
and stick her head in the car
the motor's running, she already know the money's in her
slide

we throwin rocks and garbage cans
barry draggn the motherfucker out

stomp
bompa dee dee da, and run your heaviest
game,
baby, baby, take
it take it,

run on way,

baby, baby, take it
take it, baby

run on way,

money on the ground

blood on the ground

the first step

we protects
provides

the example
plain

when the sun
come up

again

Five Father Divine Women Circling a cadillac
on the Last Day of the Year 1966

Where are you in the snow, ghost, looking at jewels
and lips, ghost, are you near us now, in hover
in a dance air, the red hair of ghost wind wraps you
near the cadillac and the ladies preparing their trip
to daddy's shrine. Steps clean. Snow pushed in the gutter.
Horn blowing for a late one to appear. The old hobbler, rushing
down the steps. You know what they do when they get there ghost
you know down in philly how they dance around a bench
cadillac breathing grey smoke on the ice, ladies assembled
crossing old bent legs. Ghost are you near us, happy or sad,
Ghost, ghost, this is the last day of the year, ghost I love you
anyway, even if you mean us harm, i know you dont,

the ladies pulld off in their cadillac
theyll be dead like you very soon
contact
broken
with
the living, the other ladies
cadillac riders in their fading youth

The Calling Together

of the tribe of the
tribes
to be the
tribe
the old strong people
nobody thought
of messing
with

If we call ourselves
together
to be the strength
of one
character
the black fist
will work
out
into
an
angel

You want to know how much stuff
You could do? How much you could build
or create? How far you could stretch
the party in your brain
the health in your soul
to be funkin' up an down
all the streets
                in the
                        universe
                like the shaking air

                Be somebody Beautiful
                Be Black and Open
                Reach for God

                                        And succeed
                                        in your life world heaven
                                        will scream at you
                                        to enter, enter Black Man
                                        bathe in Blackness

Energies exploding
Black World Renewed
Sparks! Stars! Eyes!
Huge Holocausts of Heaven
Burning down the white man's world
Holy Ashes!!!

Let the rains melt them into rivers.
And the new people naked bathe themselves
And look upon the life to come as the heaven
                            we
                            seek

                                        Sonni Weusi Akbar
                                        SF July 1967

Funeral Poem

In death the dead remember their spirit
selves and be with us in spirit for now
and here and not with us but near us forever
as they are
in their mist skin
in their fire, or air, or watery
substance
the dead are
with us always
not as the dead
but as the breath
not as the husk
but as the seed
they live
other places
they take
other faces
they are the living
they are the evolved beings

my love with them, is going, never
to leave me, dear lady i lost you
young child you are tomorrow
wait for me on the other side of appearance
wait for me near wet evening and dancing
near drums
and soft laughing
you are a voice in my self
a night a day a moment an eternity
a bright burst of light and holiness

were
ever

Night

In the rain
she was singing
"I-eee

want

some

one

to

hooooooooo-uld

m . . .

&passed

Stirling Street September

(for Sylvia)

I CAN BE THE BEAUTIFUL BLACK MAN
because I am
the beautiful black man, and you, girl, child nightlove,
you are beautiful
too.
We are something, the two of us
the people love us for being
though they may call us out our
name, they love our strength
in the midst of, quiet, at the peak of,
violence, for the sake of, at the lust of
pure life, WE WORSHIP THE SUN,

We are strange in a way because we know
who we are. Black beings passing through
a tortured passage of flesh.

Note to America

You cannot hurt
Muhammud Ali, and stay
alive

See it clearly
and you will see
yourself
clear
the gigantic shadow
of the world
the reality the existence of reality

see clearly and that's what you will see yourself and god
no different
looking
as a shadow substance a portion of all
of every thing
simply
god
a whole

african shores with cool blue sudsy waves
graham cracker sweet sand and sun to lay out in
thinking of colors bathing in the essence of hot green
hot blue hot
brown hot shore odor
perfume of blackness

still staring
hypnotized by the silence inside your head

the many scenes unroll an endless picture scroll
of doing thinking feeling being
forever endless in the instant
we lean transformed into energy
transformed into blurrd motion
all that is transformed specks of fire
memory itself burning through grey saints
talking ages years babbling through themselves
specks of greyness fire steams minutely seaheaven
atompeople spiders webbed finger buddhas ascending each second
ascending, falling, being murdered, receiving enlightenment
dot things fasting, invisible beings passing into grey gas, or back
into invisible beings, souls on the loose, magnified terror thrown from the
ant's eye . . . trillions of hands . . . trillions of "feet" . . . trillions of "poems" . . .
trillions and trillions of all the every things . . . trillions of planets . . .
trillions and trillions of heroes and devils only one God . . . only only One
God . . . is all that all them trillions . . . all them dots and inches and specks
and minutes . . . and voids . . . and universes all anything anything could imagine
resolved in the silent beating of forever divinity

you are a portion of this
you are the total jazzman
a note on the horn

you are the total fingering
the jawshaking happy hipster waggling at the edge of the stage
you are the perfection the wisdom of the right shaped note-breath-heart
burning all of the world
the universe is close to your lips
blow it out

180

For All Matter

1.

The black man is not worried yet. He thinks
he has
control.
He thinks he knows God through and through and bides his
time tracks of my tears style
or is the anyway ooooommmmmmm
of his sweet orange shirt wearing
self. He can be down
beat or locked between the devil's
thighs New Star
shooting into cold oblivion

He is not worried, among the congolene crosses
and limping addicts of dumbness, the turnaways
and hopeless cases, the country boys leaned against
department stores sweater tucked in they pants, hat turned
around, who know enough to swallow european urine for as long as there's that
to swallow, saying i know enough, i am enough
the buildings shake
a wind did it
windows glisten 20 stories above the earth
the sun did it
the black man looking at his reflection
in the indescribable foulness of American

definition. Does he see his isolated bullshit.
Does he see himself connected with the spirit of all faith
the animating gesture, work out baby hipster of the planet
the grace, does he see
the liar does not know enough to say bout
the things this black man might have seen.
Where the sun reflects the rime and stammer of emotion.
heat rising off the cooled out foreheads of the operated upon.
The programmed move back and forth in suits and autos wishing upon the
blankness. the bright spots in back of them are worlds evolving, humans
ascending through their poisonclouds.

The black man at the corner he does not want to be anybody else.
And yet the self that praises his silence is never allowed to become.
The dancing shit is dancing shit in the hand of a god it would be the dancing
shit of the world being changed to the dancing shit, the world being changed
to the praying, to the shaping the fasting the emotional depth of god's reason.

2.

The will to be in tune
the depth of god
the will of wills thunder and rain
silence throws light and decision
to be in
tune
with
God.
To be under every minute of every minute
and listening to the breathing of everything that breathes

to be alone with the God of creation the

holy nuance

is all beings.

Is the melody, and rhythm

of

the dancing

shit

itself.

Are their blues singers in russia?

Spies are found wanting. They wanted
in line, on the snow, a love to get high
with, and not, the line, a lie, a circling
tone of merciless involvement, the pushing, the
stomping, an image of green space was what the spy
wanted, standing there being shoved and hurled around
by his nostrils. They cold nights, after waiting, and
worse mornings. When the girls go by, and the lights go off
and on, to forget the clocks, and the counting of cobblestones
to keep pure cellar static off his back. The li'l darling, holding
'is wee wee he gotta pee, a little run down he leg. He pants soiled,
the wind freezed that part of his leg that wanted love most

We stand for tragic emblems when we return to the pros and cons
of the world. The shielding, for nothing, God's contradictions we
speak about as if we knew something, or could feel past what we
describe, and enter the new forms of being. See the door and enter,
get in out of the snow, the watermoccasins, and stuff, mud he
carried around in his mouth, or on the ground up to his ankles,
it'll get stupid or boring. So much, so much, to prepare a proper

184

A jew on the corner was thinking
of bargains. A dog, out back
did not start yet, howling, puny words,
barking in sorrow, a boat, for the spy's family to ride in
while they watched a sinking image of the world, and the spy's death
in snow they could really dig as beautiful or cool or somewhere else,
or just grimy lace curtains would make them hang against the boat's window
dreaming of God. The disappointment would come
after they opened their mouths, or version last
would come, and coparmies would salute the jewish dog
barking the rhythms of embezzled deserts.

We are all spies for god.

We can get betrayed. We ask for it, we ask
so much. And expect the fire the sun set the horizon
to slide through human speech dancing our future dimensions.
We expect some real shit. We expect to love all the things
somebody runs down to us. We want things, and are locked here, to the earth,
by pussy chains, or money chains, or personal indulgence chains, lies, weak
phone calls, attempts to fly when we know good and fucking well we can't and even
the nerve to get mad, and walk around pretending we are huge magnets for the
most beautiful force in the universe. And we are, but not in the image of wind
spreading the grass, or brown grass dying from a sudden snow, near the unemployment office where the spy stands trying to remember just why he wanted to
be the kinda spy he was

cops

flyolfloyd, i kno from barringer,
he used to be the daredevil sax playing
lover of the old sod, near the hip park
where they threw you in, he, with some others,
notably Allen Polite, was a lover, and smooth as anything blowin
in them parts, in that town, in that time
he weighs 400 now
and threatens junkies
on Howard Street, calling them by first or nick
names, really scaring the piss out of them, being
"a nice guy" and all his killings being accidental.
Bowleg Otis played football but was always a prick
he made detective by arresting a dude he knew all his life,
he waited in the cold counting white folks' smiles. Lenny
drives a panel truck, Leon parkd in front of the city hospital
bullshitting, but he'd split yr head. He was a bad catcher w/
Baxter Terrace, you slide home head first you get messed up
strong as a bitch. Herbert Friday, beat up Barry one night,
Herbie was a funnytime cat never played anything. Cats used to
pop his sister. You wanna stand in front of a bar, with a gun
pointed at you? You wanna try to remember why you liked somebody
while the bullet comes. Shit.

Prettyditty

Who were the guys
who wrote, who winced around
and thought
about
things? Oh, the kind of cats, you know wobbling
through a crowd full of electric
identifications, and the blessings
of the planets? who said that, howd
you get in this bar, what are you a
smart dude, with his hair some kind
a funny way, with his hand to prop
ersition the enemies of grace amen
music drowns us sit down anyway you
louse, and you got a story, i got
one he got one, and that bitch way cross
there,
she gott
a mother
fucker.

The Test

They drive us
against
the wall white
people
do, against
our natures
free and easy atoms
of peaceful loving
ness. Beautiful things. Our sign permits
of the upward gaze. Toward heaven, or haven, in
the spirit reach of black strength, up soaring,
like Gods we are in hell, fallen, pulling now
against the gravity of the evil one himself.
Black streak from sun power. We are Gods, Gods,
flying in black space. And now we are in Hell.
You see the fire and death. (The jew enters,
with desert pouch and four italian mobster
cops. Their God is a simple one. He hangs over the earth
with his dripping piles killing the trees. He enters,
to force us into crazyhouses and caskets. The bastard
enters, he enters, with four dragons, fatsos full of television
spaghetti, which is chinese anyway, he enters, with his pulpish
eyes, and disgusting habits. He enters. With them. He enters. The
bastard enters.) You see
dead niggers wallowing in the street. You see
the celebration of ignorance and ugliness. This
is the white man's image. This is what hell is.

Vowels 2

Freeeeeeeeeeeeeee

Freeeeeeeeeeeeeee

Freeeeeeeeeeeeeee   EEE EEE EEE
    EEE EEE EEE

    EEE EEE EEE
    EEE EEE EEE

Freeeeeeeeeeeeeee   BURST

Bodys moving in the light   BURST

BODYS MOVING
BODYS MOVING

FREEEEEEEEEEEEEEEEEEEEEEEE EEEEE

BODYS MOVING
BODYS MOVING

                    BURST

                    BURST

                    EEE EEE
                    EEE EEE

BODYSMOVING SOUNDS BEATS AROUND IT BEAT EEEEEE FREEE EEEEE
BODYS MOVING FREEEEEE

                    BURST

                    BURST

                    BURST

                    BURST

                    BURST

(The heart opens in vision upon itself
this is the moving beating heart of the world
be redness in the blood
blueness in the sky
hardness in the ground

                    BURST

& stay

BURST
BURST
BURST

    (& stay

       your body's moving now
       yes your body's moving
       preach preach preach
       your body's moving
       preach

          BURST
            preach
              BURST
                preach
                  BURST
                    PREACH
                    PREACH
                    PREACH

Burst BURST Burst BURST

Body's moving mind is soul is spirit is is the place

the energy

   the force

191

Sacred Chant for the Return of Black Spirit and Power

Ohhh break love with white things.
Ohhh, Ohhh break break break let it roll down.

Let it kill, let it kill, let the thing you are destroy
let it murder, and dance, and kill. Ohhh OhhhOhhh break
the white thing. Let it dangle dead. Let it rot like nature needs.

MMMMMMMMMMM

MMMMMMMMMM . . . OOOOOOOOOO . . . DeathFiddle
                                    Claw life from space
                                    Time

                                    Cries inside bleeds the word

The sacred Word

Evilout. Evilin. Evil Evil
White evil, god good, break love. Evil Scream.

Work smoke-blood steams out thick bushes.
We lay high and meditating on white evil.
We are destroying it. They die in the streets.
Look they clutch their throats. Aggggg. Stab him.
Aggggggg.
MMMMMMMM
OOOOOOOO

Death music reach us.
Bring us back our strength.

To turn their evil backwards
is to
live.

The World Is Full of Remarkable Things

(for little Bumi)

Quick Night
easy warmth
The girlmother lies next to me
breathing
coughing
sighing
at my absence. Bird Plane
Flying near Mecca
Sun sight warm air
through
my air foils. Womanchild
turns
lays her head
on my
stomach. Night aches
acts
Niggers rage

down the street. (Air
Pocket, sinks
us. She lady
angel brings
her self
to touch me
grains & grass & long
silences, the dark
ness my natural
element, in
warm black skin
I love &
understand
things. Sails
cries these
moans, pushed

from her by my
weight, her legs
spreading wrapping
secure the spirit
in her.
        We begin our
ritual breathing
flex the soul clean
out, her eyes slide
into   dreams

Television Lovers Cannot Help Me

I am the final soul
of my dreamed
reality. It all
works. I sit
in an electric
chair
dreaming
of my youth.

At the pt.
where the dreams
meet, beat into each other
by the passage
of time

Bumi

I forgotten who
I is
I wanted to be some body
and lost it
I lost my self
I *lost love*
I left a girl
  dying
I see her
  all the time
I dont know
  what
  to do
   I
  wish my mind
  wd stay here

Dust ocean a city
faces like napkins
fire hydrants catch
them I cd walk
if I want to
I used to run
I can sing a little
bit but that still
don't say I can heal
or bring back
the dead

From the Egyptian

I will slaughter
the enemies
of my father
I will slay those
who have blinded
him.

I will slaughter
the
enemies
of my
father
I will slay those
who have
blinded
him

To blind int race the slur tore slaw tearing
the eys, ice cold broatish maggots babble-tering
battering the ice
kaltenborn machine gunned
avie's ave livingston presumed
trapped, sapped, capped by the living
nigger, traits for the traitorous nigger doctors
whose asses and stomachs cost more than telephones

cripple pipple
mine but cripple babbar
ooni
mc-rout and death cruel murder
rip their uniforms off and stomp feet in their throat
smash them, rip their bellies, bash the heads with stoned
niggers sailing across the world, broome street squadron
parked near West Kinney, when the light changes they leap
at the cars, the troats, yelling, tho, burd ies eyes tap
squish under mad tree crus crunch-oo good, my eyes, my baby
the face, goerge, oh god, please i didn't i didnt the nigger

cop bop stamp, his gun, fuck you, shit, AEEEERRRRRR, twist
blues hill rope yall mixd uuuh, ummuuua. the. ouaff. We. Ow
god, that woman i we were in the egyptian bar, looked at her,
the huge art object of destruction

Great thing
Great great thing
    great thing
        GREAAAAT
               Gre-e(a)t thing great thing great great thing
dirty fucking shit HEYAIEEE great scraping fuckin head yes diggair
dutair moto'freakin scrashteemash
                        car bashed into house fat legs
                   upside down, and smashed bloody JESUS
              what'll we do, lets geh-uh ohh ra-ze ra-ze
                I will slaughter the enemies of my father
                I will slay those who have blinded him.

Black People: This Is Our Destiny

The road runs straight with no turning, the circle
runs complete as it is in the storm of peace, the all
embraced embracing in the circle complete turning road
straight like a burning straight with the circle complete
as in a peaceful storm, the elements, the niggers' voices
harmonized with creation on a peak in the holy black man's
eyes that we rise, whose race is only direction up, where
we go to meet the realization of makers knowing who we are
and the war in our hearts but the purity of the holy world
that we long for, knowing how to live, and what life is, and
who God is, and the many revolutions we must spin through in our
seven adventures in the endlessness of all existing feeling, all
existing forms of life, the gases, the plants, the ghost minerals
the spirits the souls the light in the stillness where the storm
the glow the nothing in God is complete except there is nothing
to be incomplete the pulse and change of rhythm, blown flight
to be anything at all . . . vibration holy nuance beating against
itself, a rhythm a playing re-understood now by one of the 1st race
the primitives the first men who evolve again to civilize the
world

Part of The Doctrine

RAISE THE RACE RAISE THE RAYS THE RAZE RAISE IT RACE RAISE
ITSELF RAISE THE RAYS OF THE SUNS RACE TO RAISE IN THE RAZE
OF THIS TIME AND THIS PLACE FOR THE NEXT, AND THE NEXT RACE
OURSELVES TO EMERGE BURNING ALL INERT GASES GASSED AT THE
GOD OF GUARDING THE GUARDIANS OF GOD WHO WE ARE GOD IS
WHO WE RAISE OUR SELVES WHO WE HOVER IN AND ARE RAISED
ABOVE OUR BODIES AND MACHINES THOSE WHO ARE WITHOUT GOD
WHO HAVE LOST THE SPIRITUAL PRINCIPAL OF THEIR LIVES ARE
NOT RAISED AND THEIR RACE IS TO THEIR NATURAL DEATHS NO MATTER
HOW UN-NATURAL, WITHOUT SPIRIT WITHOUT THE CLIMB THROUGH SPACE
TO THE SEVENTH PRINCIPLE WITHOUT THE PURE AND PURITY OF, THE
SPIRIT. TO RAISE THE EYES TO RAISE THE RACE AND THE RAYS OF
OUR HOT SAVAGE GODS WHO DISAPPEARED TO REAPPEAR IN THE BODY
IN THE ARM MOVE THROUGH THE GOD OF THE HEAVEN OF GOD WHERE
WE RAISE THE RACE AND THE FACE THROUGH THE EYE OF SPACE
TO RAISE AND THE RAYS OF THE RACE WILL RETURN THROUGH ALL SPACE
TO GOD TO GOD TO GOD TO GOD TO GOD TO GOD TO GOD, GOD GOD GOD
GOD GOD GOD GOD GOD GOD GOD GOD GOD GOD GOD GOD GOD GOD GOD
GOD GOD GOD GODGODGODGODGODGODGODGODGODGODGODGODGODGODGOD
GODGODGODGODGODGODGODGODGODGODGODGODGODGODGODGODGODGODGOD

To Suns raise, to raise the sons and the old heat of our truth
and passage through the secret doctrinaire universe. Through
God. We are raised and the race is a sun sons suns sons burst
out of heaven to be god in the race of our raise through perfection.

Human to Spirit
Humanism
for animals. Cut the pig
a
loose. *To You*
man
from all fours
from cold caves
to higher forms
humans
human being, emerge
from cavelight television
murder heart funky duck
the deadeye ruler dead
for oceans drying aeons

Human
to spirit. We are humans
reaching spirit. Soul our
souls
reacher
souls
reacher reaching thru a soul
action of
reaching
reacher a
soul
husk of body pass
away
husk of meat & pus
(pass)
away
humans
We are humans have been
humans
beings

passing a
way

Reaching
Changing
Being

Humanism for Animals
Hey for Animals
Pigs in the
               polycrazy nausea
               narcissistic bitches
               in phobia. Hey
pink meaty eaters raneemals
slobbereating cavenalistic
to humans
they aspire

to be humans   will
we let
them (to humans
Meat for humans?
Meat for eaters of flesh.
They aspire
to being
human

Will we let them
be
humans?

Humanism
for animals. They
should put their paws
together, clean their
jowly bloody teeth
and pray
to humans.

Humanism
for animals. We shd
turn them into humans?
The fire will.
                    (OH but!

The fire will.
Fire of the humanistic change
Smoke of the humans
We are humans
turning
to spirit.
Humanism
for animals.

Reach
humanism animals
in the flame we throw
upon you
reach
in the Red agony burning
our souls reach
we burn inside
transform the world
spiritual
reaching
of
humans

We are reaching
as God for God
as human
knowing
spirit

We leave
the humans
We find

the humanity
Humanism
for animals
Spiritism
for Humans
Reach
Brother
Reach

The Black Man is making new Gods

Atheist jews double crossers stole our secrets crossed
the white desert white to spill them and
turn into wops and bulgarians.
The Fag's Death
they give us on a cross. To Worship. Our dead selves
in disguise. They give us
to worship
a dead jew
and not ourselves
chained to the bounties
of inhuman
mad chains of
dead jews
and their wishes
and their escape
with our power
with our secrets and knowledge
they turn into loud signs
advertising empty factories
the empty jew
betrays us, as he does
hanging stupidly
from a cross, in an oven, the pantomime
of our torture,
so clearly, cinemascope the jews do it
big, hail the whiteness of their
waking up unhip
now
ties
with the black holy ghost
who created them
from the dirt on a bum hunch
the shit
would be useful.

These robots drag a robot

in the image of themselves, to be
ourselves, serving their dirty
image. Selling fried potatoes
and people, the little arty bastards
talking arithmetic they sucked from the arab's
head.
Suck you pricks. The best is yet to come. On how
we beat you
and killed you
and tied you up.
And marked this specimen
"Dangerous Germ
Culture." And put you back
in a cold box.

Tele/vision

In the beginning of my love wild hearts and trees. Greenness. The waves
at the end of the street. Dynamite proposals. To be a man,
or a white thing crawling through nuns dreams. In
the beginning of my heart we walked and rode
motorcycles into each other, killing each other,
fucked japs, in the beginning, and were sammy davis
for allen ginsbergs frank sinatra. the beginning,
of the alien. of the path back to my self. the cold
illinois skeltons of dostoevski. in the track crossing,
in the movie feeling (that's saturday evening culture
for the blind). I hurt myself. I struck and stabbed
and wounded my own gentle flesh. I began. This sliding
talking pictures of old relatives sudden heroes who were
dead spitos of the winded-up-leroy heading down belmont avenue

thinking he was grey. James Edward's nose was too ugly hunched open like that. And the other dude, the doctor, calling him dirty names invisible kike of the mind. In the beginning I was not born but plotted They came north to make me. Brain sparks and the cold cinder wheel. Sharpened. Remembering. African dances for tarzan, until the jungle pots boil darkness and the hot sun fashions it into black heroes. Run out of the south, from falling down wells, from cursing in my sleep, and the dead fall through the space "of all endeavor." Bullshit, I limped along with the rest of the niggers, and was beautiful then to invisible greys. They found me, found each at the end of the long slaughter house. Who will save the jesusnigger? Who will come back smiling and licking him silent knowledge. Who will be the final coming attraction and beautiful character actor of my bonafide creation? The me's of it. The strong I's. Yell. They. CRAAAAAAAYYYY YYYYYYYYYYVE to good faith blessing. Ahhh. The nature. The smell. I am whole.

I am whole.

Plenty

Invisible reality like twist thrush ball jamming in
the heavens, invisible strength there is no caution in
God's head. It expands like the magnificence of breath
Everything is space and a home. All life exists were
a plant any thing. We are no thing, we are every space
of living. We are flying without airplanes, cooking
without stoves. Touch God and know him, look into
your screaming brain. In those chambers the real way lurks
in the shadow of your meaningless desires. The
real breadth of where we move toward, the perfection
of space.

Karma

A call on the telephone, lifting it
I say Aw, I know you, Cranston, the inventor
of Prick Soup. He sez no he's not that person
he's another thing, another reconnection with
marching up and down in the sun in puerto rico
or eating benzedrine gulping it up like horseshit
in the back of the speeding paddy wagon. He is an
American he "re-iterates," and his breathing scalds
the walls around the telephone. He has some money
he sounds like, he has trouble coming, he sounds like, he
wants to know what happened to his wife that time in Preston Foster's
sitting room. You know the lights were out, and his sound was
lights out in Preston Foster's sitting room, and still I did not
have his name he said it anyway, it was ringing ringing, round-
in-circles, ringing, he name he said I think from what i feel now
sd he name was round-in-ringing-circles, back, o devilsucker o, bad bad
mans

Indians. Ride. Hey. Sun's red
dust sprinkled lights moving rock
ahead the slopes of years and time
beating back, water waves snow, in
skin and smokes circling up through
heavy falls. Skins. Silent woman love
me. Indian. Rides. Hey. Night silhouette.
Rides. We cannot make a tongue like that wideness
and fast horse sky. Free, and moving quick. Slide down
to leaps warmth and smokes like eyes big and pretty. Fixed
free chasm 1000 feet spread out and moving, quick. Slide down
the silent woman waits. Her Hands want you, fast, free, wide,
fixed in moving space millions of beautiful shocks she moves
across to pull you. Indians.
                    Indians. Hey.
                    Ride, as natural warriors

of the lord. God
touch me in clear
heaven. In free clean
skies, moving quick. A warm wet tongue
our boats put out in
take me, bighip girl,
pull me in your dazzle.

Indians. Hey.

Ride. As colored ghosts
and blue jewel feather
touch me, girl and warrior.

That tongue is lost. That was is dead. That heaven sky and God
is beaten, perished from
all warm colored people
trying to live their spiritual
lives.

On 4th Ave Seattle, a twentysix year old king
pulls roaches off his balls. A drunken foam
spits over his gums. On a park bench, young nigger,
a colored king dies a hundred years.

Indians. Hey.
We see a man getting into his "people car."
He is clean bald and blind. He is white
and "healthy." Clothed in the rent of the planet.

Tonight at 11:30, he will return from his electric cave
to pay homage to the warriors.

                          Passing close,
              he will stop (his old lady cold thighed before
                            the eye, she sleeps, connected)

                                              approach that chief

and kneel, silently
making his homage, his thin lips,
seeking strength from the young chief's
dick

Election Day—2

The lies of young boys are to be heard about, or read about, or perhaps
generally tolerated, but the lies of an old man. Of a man growing bald
and fat. These are the lies of death. And the cloak of death they spread.
We can die from them. Like choked by underbrush, heavy weeds. We see him.
Pull the election lever, and men die in Graystone, electrocuted, or are
beat to death on the corners of dirty cities. By heroes. These are the
killers' heroes. Wd that they were our own. And not the mad races killing
us. We have a nigger in a cape and cloak. Flying above the shacks and whores.
he has just won an election. A wop is his godfather. Praise Wop from whom
all blessing flow. The nigger edges sidewise in the light breeze, his fingers
scraping nervously in his palms. He has had visions. With commercials. Change
rattles in his pockets. He is high up. Look, he signals. Turns, backup, for
cheers. He swoops. The Wop is waving. Wave Wop. He swoops, he has a metal
mother-sister, loves him, made him from scrap iron. Taught him to fly. Wave
Metal sister. Grump and waddle. Grouch at heaven, love and God. Metal woman
wave the nigger in. He sails. Wopwaves. Crowds of neckless italians whistle
and tell jokes. Leaving rings around the East River. They swim with the goods.
"Hello, this is Heroin Plant Sardinia, How many bags you want Jefe?"
He is leading us, through the phonecalls and shootups. He is flying ahead,
giving being losing a head. I love him. He is made of iron and is steered
by a huge white joint. Fly commissioner. He loves us. We are his people.
Look
he waves and sails. Tho the breeze is wind is gale and stiff and turns him

213

back and up against his will. Wave will. And sister ironhole. And neckless ton of wop. Wave. Look. He loves and beckons to us. He is proceeded far ahead, in purple fading rheumatic wings, by the aluminum coon. Long dead, but pushed in the same heavy storm. His dry fly wings batting sideways useless, lips eyes fingers squeezing shut and open wings flaking loose in the wind. He is the old leader killed from booze and electricity. He is The Flag, and turns his votes into pizzerias. The "new man" has a guideline leads from alum to him, from ass to nose, and through the spine, and tied with chains to the white quivering dick shoved halfway up his ass, its tip like an enormous fishmouth is the victorious candidate's tongue. Talk vic torious candidate, when you land, or while you fly. Talk, and wave. We moving now. We see all of you hovering above us, gods of the unflushed commode.

Victorious candidate, we are your lowly slovenly ignorant people, and we need no help. We are merely the scorekeepers for your hip enterprises. Oh, victorious roundshouldered nigger candidate
daughter of a victorious roundshouldered nigger
mother-father. We are no
bodies. We are no merit.
We are to be used and killed
and lied to. Don't mind us, oh
victorious roundshouldered imitation
whiteman, fly onin your vacuum packed commode, do not fear us, we are garbage, we are filth, listen to our dirty mouths, look at our loud clothes and bad grammar. We are indeed scum, yr honor, lock us up. We aint shit, baby. We aint nothin. Don't mind us, partner, jus go on head, where you gon' go. All we can do is watch, That's all my man, just watch, and maybe pray

214

Allegro con rocks

A morning poem
is to dig any new
change, inside
the skull's hairy
dynamism. From depths
the heights and colors
wept and songs blue
mus
ic
poun
supon
what are turning crazy
windows
when the soldiers' trucks
have
gone.

This morning in Newark New Jersey
there is too much snow
in the ground soul
of the lodge. The wives
and meat be-ers'
thighs are bumpy
winter program

the morning poem
will be their atti
tude&
alti
tude

their version
of being
seen.

And what a scene Mis
der
Kur

.o
saw
her!
A beautiful
babe,
but too much
lip.

Unquote, the trees and shit
the streets
and shit
covered
covered completely
by cold blasts
of white universe

leroy

I wanted to know my mother when she sat
looking sad across the campus in the late 20's
into the future of the soul, there were black angels
straining above her head, carrying life from our ancestors,
and knowledge, and the strong nigger feeling. She sat
(in that photo in the yearbook I showed Vashti) getting into
new blues, from the old ones, the trips and passions
showered on her by her own. Hypnotizing me, from so far
ago, from that vantage of knowledge passed on to her passed on
to me and all the other black people of our time.
When I die, the consciousness I carry I will to
black people. May they pick me apart and take the
useful parts, the sweet meat of my feelings. And leave
the bitter bullshit rotten white parts
alone.

Eyes and Ears of the World

The rules of the life, are the rules. Here, we
find a "gentlmen" dressed in green moralities. Green
because not old white wilted man, television trails
the toilet of their breath. These gentlemen. Ever
see fags drinking tea in India on leather
toadstools?

The colors of the universe
beginning with blue:

    true road faith and some speed.
    blue things are real. And speed.
    the blue of calendars, their calm
    seas and apostles walking around
    with staffs preaching in the tourist
    traps. A few would be bluer, even
    black blue to carry a cross
    for the doomed jew (scholars
    would remark) like crispus attucks
    whom the "goodhair/badhairs" have
    found out was up tight with whitey
    for having made the first yankee
    gungadin move.

the blues of the universe
beginning with colored:

    we are here and stay to smile, finally.
    We know too much to blow. The styles

yet on Beacon Street. Breathe that heavy love. Death of our own doing. To be marching cross a wooden bridge in new england, brides the skeleton. We hate it. We see it. The fame. That criss cross. So they march down broad street whistling shortbrimmed niggers, brains fanned by the propellers of formal jehovah. Even blessed in the crackerdome. All Praise The Congealed Vomit In Lyndon Johnson's Mouth! That it rattles at our progress toward understanding. For Crispus Attucks was not even a nigger, for being talked about by beady eyes so tough. Forget it. And love him to be misunderstood so, and on Sunday.

The rules
of the life.
The colors
of the universe.
Beginning with what we remember. The taste.
All the small variances of nature. That we feel forever, even dying locked in sciencefiction suits, the withered skulls of an ancient race. All the universes, and all their implications. I will not march to celebrate Crispus Attucks dying for white men. Nor will I celebrate the deaths of my brothers misguided, butchered by brothers for the unemployment rate, and for prosperity. The people who need killing are standing next to us in the television yaks or selling us automobiles. Hubert Humphries is a warcriminal! Why him, just 12 days before valentine's day? All the love! The lace and criminal pink. The bows and chocolate

bunnies eaten by big teeth. "Hubert Humphries is not even to blame."
Let Hubert Humphries remain obscure forever, except for this poem
which uses him as the superwhitey because nobody hates him enough.
This is to point out that he deserves in his balding gentilities
to be hated hunted and killed. Just 12 days before valentine's day.

For the lace bunnies and comic ladybabies dingling through the air.
And the air of this time and this place is a bad smell song.
The bunnies. Reach. Robots. Chase. Death. Destruction. Heathenhelp
they walk their nights in the sweat of evil. Of jewish "wickedness"
and slippery fingers. So even art is anonymous if you can wipe out
the world and be competent, even brilliant, the prosperity is death

Is Worth It
Is we-my-they call ranstung cripple hills the wind of crashing
cars. Fall out roll dying. Hello Mr. Humphries in India. Dead Cow
culture. Neat editorials. The yellow pages. To find anything.
Except Mr. Humphries and Mrs. Humphries. Toxic Frank Morgan
Wizards. Deadly Billy Burke. Gold shoes, and straight white light
of God from the radio. Shining on the rug. Dead people ankles
stick out under the couches. My mother is babbling. My father
is babbling. My woman is babbling. I'm babbling. Caught lost
in the knife-edge jellyballs of the vicepresident's needs.

Sisters in the Fog

The rewards of love
are multifaced. They'll change
you are changed and worn and real.
So the spikes of sun wont kill you
if you're wrong, grow old in the ease
of your brothers blood, and be plain dumb niggers
with the only quality truly transferable among humans,
stupidity. There are fights in the streets with the cops
and a brother is wounded and jailed. His wife screams curses
at life, the time, the motion, god, all beauty, and her wounded
self. Would that that self would disappear and she grow more beautiful
than the fake virgin of the christians, Mary Marvel, whose antics invented
cuckoldry as hip in the sacred texts of the beasts. Would that we would
all become what the dream of reality insists we can become.

Race

The madness
of Cane, striked
the dumb world, agin
striked it,
drove it,
bangbanged it, with the misery
of its history, its out of sight piles
of misery and hurt and deadly disorder.
It's flunkiness in the face of rulers.
It's wanting to cool itself, with excess
while grey freaks ate its mothers.

Wow.

What Who
has it become
What Who?

Whose thing are we? Can we get clear enough
to think, to see, to go to bed
with ourselves, and come
to brave black conclusions?

I with and out of it. (3 Ways) I spring out of its mouth
and it blazes above me
with black fire.

It chokes the oceans
if they mess around. It is
in the beast of its beautiful self
full of all
of us. And we stare into its messy love, with every thing
we could possibly
hope to be.

I love all the things I am and all the things you are. Bull shit life,
and its reflection, with the whole searing responsibility
to find actual
happiness.
            That we could do it. And will.
            Will it.

Distant hearts, come close
r, in the smash
of night.

Title it a smell. In the twilight of our lives, as
things. There is an Egyptian feeling come back
to cleanse us. We sail, this is holier than any
form, that it is, all forms. If we speak of
"Economics," a white man sits on his arm, listening,
dirt falling off his 19th century body. The year
of their Lord, who is now, famously
dead.
Magic Cities
begin to re/form. Our strength is in the drums,
the sinuous horns, blow forever beautiful princes, touch
the spellflash of everything, all life, and the swift go on
go off and speed. Blow forever, like the animals plants and
sun. Forever in our universe there is beauty and light, we come
back to it now. Throwing off the tons of dumb metal the beast
has strapped us in. Those Things. These refrigerators, stoves,
automobiles, airships, let us return to the reality of spirit,
to how our black ancestors predicted life should be, from the
mind and the heart, our souls like gigantic kites sweep across
the heavens, let us follow them, with our trembling love for
the world. Let us look up at each other's spirits zooming, and
enter the cities of Gods.

Planetary Exchange.

We are meat in the air. Flying into night space.
Meat complexified by evolution from the original
stuff. Re-evolved and retread, grown, bolted, hands
feet working, like they do, from slimy water, even now,
shot out the peter, through the crisscross round mileage
of speed and explosion.

I am.

Burst of the planet, burst through years I see on a hill
in electric your death and am puzzled. I am. I am. Milliards
of millions of no thing, blank, zero, indian time. To go.
And me. My feeling, and clicking brain. Zero. From nothing.
To nothing. Just speed and adventure, sensation. But truth,
real shit, where is it. I am. I am. I am. Through the dazzling
lives of the planets and stars. I am. sings.

Black People!

What about that bad short you saw last week on Frelinghuysen, or those stoves and refrigerators, record players in Sears, Bambergers, Klein's, Hahnes', Chase, and the smaller joosh enterprises? What about that bad jewelry, on Washington Street, and those couple of shops on Springfield? You know how to get it, you can get it, no money down, no money never, money dont grow on trees no way, only whitey's got it, makes it with a machine, to control you you cant steal nothin from a white man, he's already stole it he owes you anything you want, even his life. All the stores will open if you will say the magic words. The magic words are: Up against the wall mother fucker this is a stick up! Or: Smash the window at night (these are magic actions) smash the windows daytime, anytime, together, let's smash the window drag the shit from in there. No money down. No time to pay. Just take what you want. The magic dance in the street. Run up and down Broad Street niggers, take the shit you want. Take their lives if need be, but get what you want what you need. Dance up and down the streets, turn all the music up, run through the streets with music, beautiful radios on Market Street, they are brought here especially for you. Our brothers are moving all over, smashing at jellywhite faces. We must make our own World, man, our own world, and we can not do this unless the white man is dead. Let's get together and killhim my man, let's get to gather the fruit of the sun, let's make a world we want black children to grow and learn in do not let your children when they grow look in your face and curse you by pitying your tomish ways.

225